Crochet Cool

Crochet Cool

Fun Designs for Kids Ages 1 to 6

Tanya Bernard

Photography by Angel Gray

SELLERS
PUBLISHING

Published by **Sellers Publishing, Inc.**
161 John Roberts Road, South Portland, Maine 04106

Visit our Web site: www.sellerspublishing.com
E-mail: rsp@rsvp.com

Design and layout copyright © 2013 BlueRed Press Ltd
Text copyright © 2013 Tanya Bernard
Patterns and templates copyright © 2013 Tanya Bernard
Step by Step photography copyright 2013 Tanya Bernard
Final project photography copyright 2013 BlueRed Press Ltd
All rights reserved.
Design by Matt Windsor

ISBN 13: 978-1-4162-0892-1
Library of Congress Number: 2012944704

10 9 8 7 6 5 4 3 2 1

Printed and Bound in China

Contents

Difficulty Key

= Easy

= Intermediate

= Advanced

Crochet Hook Sizes		
METRIC SIZES(mm)	US SIZES	UK/ CANADIAN
2.0	-	14
2.25	B/1	13
2.5	-	12
2.75	C/2	-
3.0	-	11
3.25	D/3	10
3.5	E/4	9
3.75	F/5	-
4.0	G/6	8
4.5	7	7
5.0	H/8	6
5.5	I/9	5
6.0	J/10	4
6.5	K/10 1/2	3
7.0	-	2
8.0	L/11	0
9.0	M/13	00
10.0	N/15	000

Introduction

When my twins were born more than four years ago, I received some beautiful crochet blankets from family and friends. I have always been crafty and the gifts inspired me to learn how to crochet! When my babies were 8 months old, I found a free knit and crochet class at my local library. Once a week, I would drive to the library to learn new techniques, get help on current projects, and honestly to have a small "me" break. I was immediately "hooked" on my new hobby. It is easy to relax on the couch in the evenings once the children are in bed with a hook and yarn in hand.

As a family of five, we enjoy traveling in our RV on long weekends and a few summer trips. I am able to bring my hobby along with me while we are driving, and I always find an excuse to visit a local yarn shop wherever we go.

While following patterns was great for learning, my creativity was exploding. I began making my own patterns, mostly newborn hats, because they were the smallest projects. Once I mastered those, I moved to blankets and clothing.

Living in Florida is a fabulous life. However, since it is warm most of the year, we can't always wear the typical crochet items of hats and scarves that are very popular. I love working with soft cotton yarns and anything full of color. I hope you enjoy the patterns in this book and they inspire you to create a wardrobe of fun for all seasons, no matter where you live.

Tanya Bernard

Spring

Daisy Dress

There is nothing sweeter than a little girl in a white dress. With an adjustable bow around the waist, this dress can accommodate a few sizes by adjusting the length. I chose this cotton for its bright white color and soft touch.

Materials

- Cascade Ultra Pima 10 x 100g/220yds 100% Pima Cotton
  – Color #3728 / color name White / 3 skeins
- Small amount of Ultra Pima #3764 Sunshine (for flower middle)
- 1 small button
- Satin ribbon to weave through top
- **Hooks:** J (6mm) for flowers and H (5mm) for dress

Skill level: Advanced   **Gauge:** 8 sc = 2", 8 sc rows = 2"

Glossary of abbreviations

ch – chain
sc – single crochet
dc – double crochet
sl st – slip stitch,
sk – skip
sp – space
y/o – yarn over
hdc – half double crochet
F/O – fasten off
(#) number of stitches at end of round
* _ * to be repeated

PUFF STITCH DAISY (make 9)
Puff Stitch:

y/o, insert hook in indicated st (Picture 2) and pull up a long loop (Picture 3), repeat 3 times, y/o and pull through all 7 remaining loops on hook (Picture 4), ch 1 to lock.

Flowers will be worked with holding two strands together while crocheting. This will make a thicker, sturdier flower.
Use size J (6mm) hook.

Round 1: ch 4, sl st to form ring, 6 hdc in ring, sl st to first hdc with petal color. (Picture 1)
Round 2: *Puff Stitch in first hdc, ch 2* repeat 5 more times to form 5 puff petals.

SIZE AGES 2/3
Size H (5mm) hook
Begin by connecting flowers for neckline of dress.

5hdc in between 2 petals of first flower, *Ch 5, 5 hdc in between bottom petals of next flower* repeat 6 more times, 5 hdc between bottom petals, *5 hdc in between petals of flower* repeat 2 more times. (Picture 5)
5 hdc between top of petals, ch 2 repeat 6 more times, *5 hdc in between petals* repeat 2 more times. The neckline of dress will be open on one side and small button can be used for closure. (Picture 6)
Round 1: Begin by attaching flowers together to form long row. (Tying a knot or sl st works well.) *5 hdc over

flower, 5 hdc in ch 5 sp* repeat 7 more times, 5 hdc on top of flower, ch 25.
Round 2: 33 hdc, ch 25, sk ch 5, 44 hdc.
Round 3: 30 hdc in ch 25 sp, 33 hdc, 30 hdc in ch 25 sp, 45 hdc.
Round 4: sk first st, *5 hdc next st, sk next 3 sts* repeat 33 more times (34 shells)
Rounds 5–38: *sl st to middle of first shell, 5 dc in between next 2 shells* repeat 33 more times. (34 shells)

FOR SIZE 4/5
Continue 7 more rounds to 45 rounds.
F/O.
Weave ribbon through round 4.

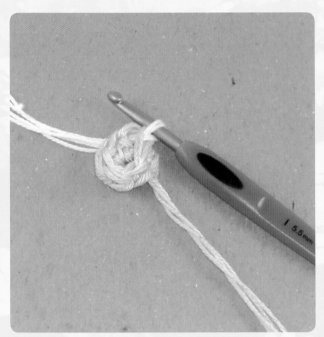

Picture 1: Sl st to 1st hdc with petal color.

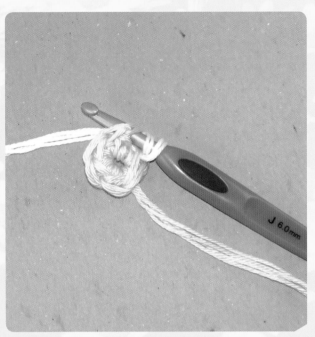

Picture 2: Y/o, insert hook in indicated st.

Picture 3: Pull up long loop.

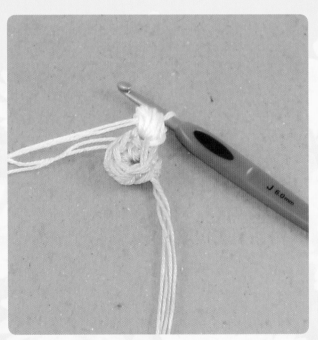

Picture 4: Repeat 3 times, y/o and pull through all 7 remaining loops on hook.

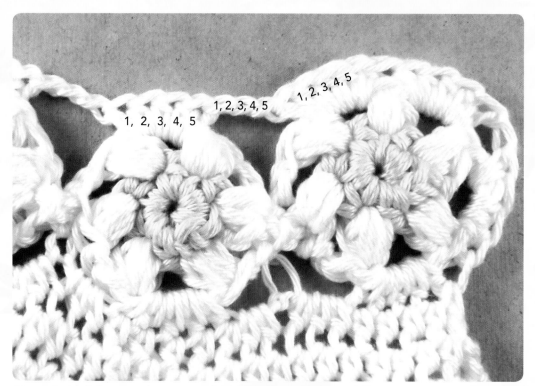

Picture 5: 5 hdc between bottom petals, 5 hdc in between petals of flower.

Picture 6: Neckline will open on one side, use small button for closure.

Striped Romper with Flower Cummerbund

Can you picture your little girl wearing this romper, playing at the park, picking flowers, or having a tea party with her favorite dolls and animals? The two shades of pink give it a great design element without adding the busy look of multicolor prints.

Materials

- Cascade Ultra Pima 10 x 100g/220yds 100% Pima Cotton
  - Color #3712 / color name Primrose / 2 skeins (Color A)
  - Color #3711 / color name China Pink / 2 skeins (Color B)
- Small amounts of additional colors used on flowers:
  - Cascade Ultra Pima #3718 Natural, #3717 Sand
- 2 small buttons for straps
- 9" X 4" Felt piece for attaching cummerbund flowers for stability
- **Hook:** H (4mm)

Skill level: Intermediate

Gauge: 10 sc = 2", 12 sc rows = 2"

Glossary of abbreviations

ch – chain
sc – single crochet
dc – double crochet
sl st – slip stitch
sk – skip
sp – space
sc dec – single crochet decrease
F/O – fasten off
y/o – yarn over
 (#) number of stitches at end
   of round
* _ * to be repeated

Helpful Tips – Color Change should happen at last y/o of previous row.
Weave strand of yarn at bottom of legs of romper and tie for ruffled effect.

SIZES AGES 1-3
SHORTS – Make two panels
Color A, ch 55, turn.
Row 1: sc in second st from hook, 53 dc across, ch 1, turn.
Rows 2–6: 54 sc across, ch 1, turn.
Rows 7–12: Color B, 54 sc across, ch 1, turn.
Rows 13–18: Color A, 54 sc across, ch 1, turn.
Rows 19–24: Color B, 54 sc across, ch 1, turn.
Rows 25–30: Color A, 54 sc across, ch 1, turn.

Rows 31–36: Color B, 54 sc across, ch 1, turn.
Rows 37–42: Color A, 54 sc across, ch 1, turn.
Rows 43–48: Color B, 54 sc across, ch 1, turn.
Rows 49–54: Color A, 54 sc across, ch 1, turn.
Rows 55–60: Color B, 54 sc across, ch 1, turn.
F/O and sew panels together.
(See Surfer Shorts photos)

TOP
Color A.
Row 1: sl st to top of shorts, 80 sc around.
Row 2: *2 sc in first st, sc in each of next 8 sts* repeat around. (90)
Row 3: *2 sc in first, sc in each of next 21 sts* repeat around. (95)
Rows 4–6: Color A, sc around. (95)
Rows 7–12: Color B, sc around. (95)
Rows 13–18: Color A, sc around. (95)
Rows 19–24: Color B, sc around. (95)
Rows 25–30: Color A, sc around. (95)
Rows 31–35: Color B, sc around. (95)

Picture 1: Mark middle of romper front and the 9th stitch to right and left.

Picture 2: To gather front, sc in first st, skip next 8 sts, sc at middle stitch marker.

SIZE AGE 3 ROMPER

Continue rows 36–40 in color A and rows 41–45 in color B.

Lay romper flat and place stitch marker in middle of front, skip 8 sts to right of middle and place stitch marker in stitch 9. Skip 8 sts to left of middle and place stitch marker in stitch 9. (Picture 1)

Row 36: sc to first st marker, sk 8 sts, sc at middle st marker, sk 8 sts, finish around with sc. (Pictures 2 and 3)

Row 37: sc around, sc through all three layers of fold. (Picture 4)

Straps

Row 1: Color A, 6 dc, ch 2, turn.
Row 2–3: 6 dc, ch 2, turn.
Row 4–6: Color B, 6 dc, ch 2, turn.
Row 7–9: Color A, 6 dc, ch 2, turn.
Row 10–12: Color B, 6 dc, ch 2, turn.
(Picture 5)

BOW

Ch 3, turn
Row 1: 2 Sc in 2nd from hook, Sc next, Ch 1, turn
Row 2: 3 Sc across, Ch 1, turn
Row 3: Sc 2nd from hook, 2 Sc next, Sc last, Ch 1, turn
Rows 4-15: 4 Sc across, Ch 1, turn
Row 16: Sc 2nd from hook, 2 Sc next, 2 Sc next, Sc last, Ch 1, turn
Rows 17-22: 6 Sc across, Ch 1, turn
Row 23: Sc 2nd from hook, Sc next, 2 Sc next, 2 Sc next, Sc last 2, Ch 1, turn
Rows 24-59: 8 Sc across, Ch 1, turn
Row 60: Sc 2nd from hook, Sc next, 2 Sc Dec over next 4 sts, Sc last 2 sts, Ch 1, turn
Rows 61-68: 6 Sc across, Ch 1, turn
Row 69: Sc Dec, Sc in next, Sc in next, Sc Dec, Ch 1, turn
Rows 70-82: 4 Sc across, Ch 1, turn
Row 83: Sc Dec, Sc, Sc, Ch 1, turn
Row 84: 3 Sc across, Ch 1, turn
Row 85: Sc Dec, Sc, Ch 1, turn
Row 86: 2 Sc across
F/O
Fold bow (Picture 6) and wrap yarn around middle. Sew to strap.

SIZE AGES 4/5
SHORTS – Make two panels
Color A. Ch 65, turn.

Row 1: sc in second st from hook, 63 dc across, ch 1, turn. (64)

Rows 2–6: 64 sc across, ch 1, turn. (64)

Rows 7–12: Color B, 64 sc across, ch 1, turn. (64)

Rows 13–18: Color A, 64 sc across, ch 1, turn. (64)

Rows 19–24: Color B, 64 sc across, ch 1, turn. (64)

Rows 25–30: Color A, 64 sc across, ch 1 turn. (64)

Rows 31–36: Color B, 64 sc across, ch 1, turn. (64)

Rows 37–42: Color A, 64 sc across, ch 1, turn. (64)

Rows 43–48: Color B, 64 sc across, ch 1, turn. (64)

Rows 49–54: Color A, 64 sc across, ch 1, turn. (64)

Rows 55–60: Color B, 64 sc across, ch 1, turn. (64)

Rows 61–66: Color A, 64 sc across, ch 1, turn. (64)

Rows 67–71: Color B, 64 sc across, ch 1, turn. (64)

F/O and sew panels together. See Surfer Shorts photos.

TOP
Color A.

Row 1: sl st to top of shorts, 90 sc around.

Row 2: *2 sc in first st, sc in each of next 8 sts* repeat around. (100)

Row 3: *2 sc in first, sc in each of next 20 sts* repeat around. (105)

Rows 4–6: Color A, sc around. (105)

Rows 7–12: Color B, sc around. (105)

Rows 13–18: Color A, sc around. (10)

Rows 19–24: Color B, sc around. (105)

Rows 25–30: Color A, sc around. (105)

Rows 31–35: Color B, sc around. (105)

Rows 36–40: Color A, sc around. (105)

Rows 41–45: Color B, sc around. (105)

Lay romper flat and place stitch marker in middle of front, skip 8 sts to right of middle and place stitch marker in stitch

Picture 3: Skip 8 sts, sc next stitch marker.

Picture 4: Sc through all three layers of fold.

9. Skip 8 sts to left of middle and place stitch marker in stitch 9. (Picture 1)
Row 46: sc to first st marker, sk 8 sts, sc at middle st marker, sk 8 sts, finish around with sc. (Pictures 2 and 3)
Row 47: sc around, sc through all three layers of fold. (Picture 4)

Straps
Row 1: Color A, 6 dc, ch 2, turn.
Row 2–3: 6 dc, ch 2, turn.
Row 4–6: Color B, 6 dc, ch 2, turn.
Row 7–9: Color A, 6 dc, ch 2, turn.
Row 10–12: Color B, 6 dc, ch 2, turn.
(Picture 5)

CUMMERBUND THREE-LAYER FLOWERS
Round 1: ch 2, 6 hdc in second st from hook.
Round 2: (sl st to first hdc, ch 2, dc, ch 2, sl St) all in first hdc st, *(sl St to next hdc, ch 2, dc, ch 2, sl st) all in hdc* repeat in each stitch around. (6 petals) F/O for small flower.

Picture 5: Place straps evenly on each side.

Picture 6: Fold bow.

Round 3: sl st to back of first petal, ch 3, *sl st to back of next petal, ch 3* repeat around for 6 ch 3 spaces.

Round 4: sl st to first ch 3 space, ch 2, 3 dc, ch 2, sl st, *(sl st to next ch 3 sp, ch 2, 3 dc, ch 2, sl st)* repeat for 6 petals F/O for medium flower.

Round 5: sl st to back of first petal, ch 5, *sl st to back of next petal, ch 5* repeat around for 6 ch 3 spaces.

Round 6: sl st to first ch 3 space, ch 2, 5 dc, ch 2, sl st, *(sl st to next ch 3 sp, ch 2, 5 dc, ch 2, sl st)* repeat for 6 petals. F/O.

Sew Flowers to 9" x 4" felt. Trim felt edges. (Picture 7)

Chain 150 for each Cummerbund strap and sew to back of felt piece. (Picture 8)

Picture 7: Sew flowers to felt for stability on cumberbund.

Picture 8: Trim felt edges and sew chains for belt.

Nautical Hoodie

2-6 years

This hooded pullover is perfect for a day of boating or as a beach cover-up. The hoodie has stitches that are open enough to keep your child cool, yet it works well as a cover-up when the breeze or the sun are too strong.

Materials

- Cascade Ultra Pima 10 x 100g/220yds 100% Pima Cotton
  - Color #3718 / color name Natural / 1 skein (Color A)
  - Color #3717 / color name Sand / 1 skein (Color B)
  - Color #3755 / color name Lipstick Red / 1 skein (Color C)
  - Color #3724 / color name Armada / 1 skein (Color D)
- **Hook:** I (5.5mm)

Skill level: Intermediate   **Gauge:** 6 sc = 2", 10 sc rows = 2"

Glossary of abbreviations

ch – chain
sc – single crochet
dc – double crochet
sl st – slip stitch
sk – skip
dc dec – double crochet decrease
F/O – fasten off
(#) number of stitches at end of round
* _ * to be repeated

Helpful Tips – By repeating 2 rows of same color, you will get a wavy design. (Picture 4)

SIZE AGES 2/3
FRONT AND BACK
Color A, ch 41.

Row 1: Color A, dc third st from hook, 3 dc, 5 sc, *5 dc, 5 sc* repeat 2 more times, ch 1, turn.

Row 2: Color A, sc second st from hook, 3 sc, 5 dc, *5 sc, 5 dc* repeat 2 more times, ch 1, turn.

Row 3: Color B, sc second st from hook, 3 sc, 5 dc, *5 sc, 5 dc* repeat 2 more times, ch 2, turn.

Row 4: Color B, dc third st from hook, 3 sc, 5 sc, *5 dc, 5 sc* repeat 2 more times, ch 2, turn.

Row 5: Color C, dc third st from hook, 3 dc, 5 sc, *5 dc, 5 sc* repeat 2 more times, ch 1, turn.

Row 6: Color C, sc second st from hook, 3 sc, 5 dc, *5 sc, 5 dc* repeat 2 more times, ch 1, turn.

Row 7: Color A, sc second st from hook, 3 sc, 5 dc, *5 sc, 5 dc* repeat 2 more times, ch 2, turn.

Row 8: Color A, dc third st from hook, 3 dc, 5 sc, *5 dc, 5 sc* repeat 2 more times, ch 2, turn.

Row 9: Color B, dc third st from hook, 3 dc, 5 sc, *5 dc, 5 sc* repeat 2 more times, ch 1, turn.

Row 10: Color B, sc second st from hook, 3 sc, 5 dc, *5 sc, 5 dc* repeat 2 more times, ch 1, turn.

Row 11: Color D, sc second st from hook, 3 sc, 5 dc, *5 sc, 5 dc* repeat 2 more times, ch 2, turn.

Row 12: Color D, dc third st from hook, 3 dc, 5 sc, *5 dc, 5 sc* repeat 2 more times, Ch 2, turn.

Row 13: Color A, dc third st from hook, 3 dc, 5 sc, *5 dc, 5 sc* repeat 2 more times, Ch 1, turn.

Row 14: Color A, sc second st from hook, 3 sc, 5 dc, *5 sc, 5 dc* repeat 2 more times, Ch 1, turn.

Row 15: Color B, sc second st from hook, 3 sc, 5 dc, *5 sc, 5 dc* repeat 2 more times, Ch 2, turn.

Row 16: Color B, dc third st from hook, 3 dc, 5 sc, *5 dc, 5 sc* repeat 2 more times, Ch 2, turn.

Row 17: Color C, dc third st from hook, 3 dc, 5 sc, *5 dc, 5 sc* repeat 2 more times, Ch 1, turn.

Row 18: Color C, sc second st from hook, 3 sc, 5 dc, *5 sc, 5 dc* repeat 2 more times, Ch 1, turn.

Row 19: Color A, sc second st from hook, 3 sc, 5 dc, *5 sc, 5 dc* repeat 2 more times, Ch 2, turn.

Row 20: Color A, dc third st from hook, 3 dc, 5 sc, *5 dc, 5 sc* repeat 2 more times, Ch 2, turn.

Row 21: Color B, dc third st from hook, 3 dc, 5 sc, *5 dc, 5 sc* repeat 2 more times, Ch 1, turn.

Row 22: Color B, sc second st from hook, 3 sc, 5 dc, *5 sc, 5 dc* repeat 2 more times, Ch 1, turn.

Row 23: Color D, sc second st from hook, 3 sc, 5 dc, *5 sc, 5 dc* repeat 2 more times, Ch 2, turn.
Row 24: Color D, dc third st from hook, 3 dc, 5 sc, *5 dc, 5 sc* repeat 2 more times, Ch 2, turn.
Row 25: Color A, dc third st from hook, 3 dc, 5 sc, *5 dc, 5 sc* repeat 2 more times, Ch 1, turn.
Row 26: Color A, sc second st from hook, 3 sc, 5 dc, *5 sc, 5 dc* repeat 2 more times, Ch 1, turn.
Row 27: Color B, sc second st from hook, 3 sc, 5 dc, *5 sc, 5 dc* repeat 2 more times, Ch 2, turn.
Row 28: Color B, dc third st from hook, 3 dc, 5 sc, *5 dc, 5 sc* repeat 2 more times, ch 2, turn.
Row 29: Color C, dc third st from hook, 3 dc, 5 sc, *5 dc, 5 sc* repeat 2 more times, Ch 1, turn.
Row 30: Color C, sc second st from hook, 3 sc, 5 dc, *5 sc, 5 dc* repeat 2 more times, Ch 1, turn.
Row 31: Color A, sc second st from hook, 3 sc, 5 dc, *5 sc, 5 dc* repeat 2 more times, Ch 2, turn.
Row 32: Color A, dc third st from hook, 3 dc, 5 sc, *5 dc, 5 sc* repeat 2 more times, Ch 2, turn.

Continue for FRONT, LEFT (or skip to BACK instructions rows 33–43).
Row 33: Color B, dc third st from hook, 3 dc, 5 sc, 5 dc, 5 sc, ch 1, turn.
Row 34: Color B, sc second st from hook, 3 sc, 5 dc, 5 sc, 5 dc, ch 1, turn.
Row 35: Color D, sc second st from hook, 3 sc, 5 dc, 5 sc, 5 dc, ch 2, turn.
Row 36: Color D, dc third st from hook, 3 dc, 5 sc, 5 dc, 5 sc, ch 2, turn.
Row 37: Color A, dc third st from hook, 3 dc, 5 sc, 5 dc, 5 sc, ch 1, turn.
Row 38: Color A, sc second st from hook, 3 sc, 5 dc, 5 sc, 5 dc, ch 1, turn.
Row 39: Color B, sc second st from hook, 3 sc, 5 dc, 5 sc, 5 dc, ch 2, turn.
Row 40: Color B, dc third st from hook, 3 dc, 5 sc, 5 dc, 5 sc, ch 2, turn.
Row 41: Color C, dc third st from hook,

3 dc, 5 sc, 5 dc, 5 sc, ch 1, turn.
Row 42: Color C, sc second st from hook, 3 sc, 5 dc, 5 sc, 5 dc, ch 1, turn.
Row 43: Color B, sc second st from hook, 3 sc, 5 dc.

For FRONT, RIGHT (Picture 1)
Row 33: Color B, sc third st from hook, 3 sc, 5 dc, 5 sc, 5 dc, ch 2, turn.
Row 34: Color B, dc second st from hook, 3 dc, 5 sc, 5 dc, 5 sc, ch 2, turn.
Row 35: Color D, dc second st from hook, 3 dc, 5 sc, 5 dc, 5 sc, ch 1, turn.
Row 36: Color D, sc third st from hook, 3 sc, 5 dc, 5 sc, 5 dc, ch 1, turn.
Row 37: Color A, sc third st from hook, 3 sc, 5 dc, 5 sc, 5 dc, ch 2, turn.
Row 38: Color A, dc second st from hook, 3 dc, 5 sc, 5 dc, 5 sc, ch 2, turn.
Row 39: Color B, dc second st from hook, 3 dc, 5 sc, 5 dc, 5 sc, ch 1, turn.
Row 40: Color B, sc third st from hook, 3 sc, 5 dc, 5 sc, 5 dc, ch 1, turn.
Row 41: Color C, sc third st from hook, 3 sc, 5 dc, 5 sc, 5 dc, ch 2, turn.
Row 42: Color C, dc second st from hook, 3 dc, 5 sc, 5 dc, 5 sc, ch 2, turn.
Row 43: Color B, dc second st from hook, 3 dc, 5 sc.
F/O.

BACK
Row 33: Color B, dc third st from hook, 3 dc, 5 sc, *5 dc, 5 sc* repeat 2 more times, ch 1, turn.
Row 34: Color B, sc second st from hook, 3 sc, 5 dc, *5 sc, 5 dc* repeat 2 more times, ch 1, turn.
Row 35: Color D, sc second st from hook, 3 sc, 5 dc, *5 sc, 5 dc* repeat 2 more times, ch 2, turn.
Row 36: Color D, dc third st from hook, 3 dc, 5 sc, *5 dc, 5 sc* repeat 2 more times, ch 2, turn.
Row 37: Color A, dc third st from hook, 3 dc, 5 sc, *5 dc, 5 sc* repeat 2 more times, ch 1, turn.
Row 38: Color A, sc second st from hook, 3 sc, 5 dc, *5 sc, 5 dc* repeat 2 more times, ch 1, turn.

Row 39: Color B, sc second st from hook, 3 sc, 5 dc, *5 sc, 5 dc* repeat 2 more times, ch 2, turn.
Row 40: Color B, dc third st from hook, 3 dc, 5 sc, *5 dc, 5 sc* repeat 2 more times, ch 2, turn.
Row 41: Color C, dc third st from hook, 3 dc, 5 sc, *5 dc, 5 sc* repeat 2 more times, ch 1, turn.
Row 42: Color C, sc second st from hook, 3 sc, 5 dc, *5 sc, 5 dc* repeat 2 more times, ch 1, turn.
Row 43: Color A, sc second st from hook, 3 sc, 5 dc, *5 sc, 5 dc* repeat 2 more times, ch 2, turn.
Stitch front and back together, leaving 5" opening for sleeve.

SLEEVE (Picture 2)
Round 1: Color D, sl st, ch 1, 35 dc around.
Round 2: Color D, dc dec, 34 dc around.
Round 3: Color D, dc dec, 33 dc around.
Round 4: Color D, dc dec, 32 dc around.
Round 5: Color D, dc dec, 31 dc around.
Rounds 6–12: Color D, 30 dc around.
Rounds 13–14: Color D, *5 sc, 5 dc* repeat 2 more times.
Rounds 15–16: Color B, *5 dc, 5 sc* repeat 2 more times.
Rounds 17–18: Color A, *5 sc, 5 dc* repeat 2 more times.
Round 19: Color C, *5 dc, 5 sc* repeat 2 more times.
Round 20: Color C, *5 sc, 5 dc* repeat 2 more times.

HOOD (Picture 3)
Row 1: Color D, sl st to collar, ch 2, 47 dc across, ch 2, turn.
Rows 2–21: 48 dc across, ch 2, turn.
Row 22: 48 dc across.
F/O.
Fold and stitch top of hood together.

SIZE AGE 4
FRONT AND BACK
Color A, ch 51.
Row 1: Color A, dc third st from hook, 3 dc, 5 sc, *5 dc, 5 sc* repeat 3 more

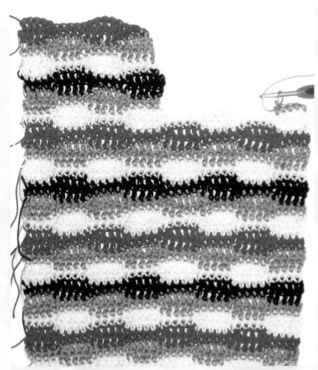

Picture 1: Attach yarn to opposite side to complete front.

Picture 2: Picture of sleeve.

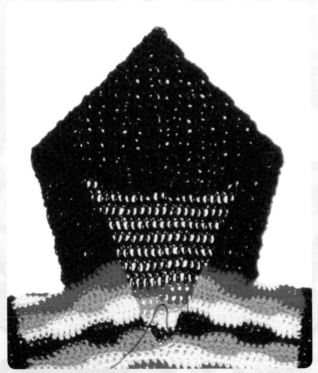

Picture 3: Fold hood and stitch top.

Picture 4: Close-up of design.

times, ch 1, turn.

Row 2: Color A, sc second st from hook, 3 sc, 5 dc, *5 sc, 5 dc* repeat 3 more times, ch 1, turn.

Row 3: Color B, sc second st from hook, 3 sc, 5 dc,*5 sc, 5 dc* repeat 3 more times, ch 2, turn.

Row 4: Color B, dc third st from hook, 3 dc, 5 sc, *5 dc, 5 sc* repeat 3 more times, ch 2, turn.

Row 5: Color C, dc third st from hook, 3 dc, 5 sc, *5 dc, 5 sc* repeat 3 more times, ch 1, turn.

Row 6: Color C, sc second st from hook, 3 sc, 5 dc, *5 sc, 5 dc* repeat 3 more times, ch 1, turn.

Row 7: Color A, sc second st from hook, 3 sc, 5 dc, *5 sc, 5 dc* repeat 3 more times, ch 2, turn.

Row 8: Color A, dc third st from hook, 3 dc, 5 sc, *5 dc, 5 sc* repeat 3 more times, ch 2, turn.

Row 9: Color B, dc third st from hook, 3 dc, 5 sc, *5 dc, 5 sc* repeat 3 more times, ch 1, turn.

Row 10: Color B, sc second st from hook, 3 sc, 5 dc, *5 sc, 5 dc* repeat 3 more times, ch 1, turn.

Row 11: Color D, sc second st from hook, 3 sc, 5 dc, *5 sc, 5 dc* repeat 3 more times, ch 2, turn.

Row 12: Color D, dc third st from hook, 3 dc, 5 sc, *5 dc, 5 sc* repeat 3 more times, ch 2, turn.

Row 13: Color A, dc third st from hook, 3 dc, 5 sc, *5 dc, 5 sc* repeat 3 more times, ch 1, turn.

Row 14: Color A, sc second st from hook, 3 sc, 5 dc, *5 sc, 5 dc* repeat 3 more times, ch 1, turn.

Row 15: Color B, sc second st from hook, 3 sc, 5 dc, *5 sc, 5 dc* repeat 3 more times, ch 2, turn.

Row 16: Color B, dc third st from hook, 3 dc, 5 sc, *5 dc, 5 sc* repeat 3 more times, ch 2, turn.

Row 17: Color C, dc third st from hook, 3 dc, 5 sc, *5 dc, 5 sc* repeat 3 more times, ch 1, turn.

Row 18: Color C, sc second st from hook, 3 sc, 5 dc, *5 sc, 5 dc* repeat 3 more times, ch 1, turn.

Row 19: Color A, sc second st from hook, 3 sc, 5 dc, *5 sc, 5 dc* repeat 3 more times, ch 2, turn.

Row 20: Color A, dc third st from hook, 3 dc, 5 sc, *5 dc, 5 sc* repeat 3 more times, ch 2, turn.

Row 21: Color B, dc third st from hook, 3 dc, 5 sc, *5 dc, 5 sc* repeat 3 more times, ch 1, turn.

Row 22: Color B, sc second st from hook, 3 sc, 5 dc, *5 sc, 5 dc* repeat 3 more times, ch 1, turn.

Row 23: Color D, sc second st from hook, 3 sc, 5 dc, *5 sc, 5 dc* repeat 3 more times, ch 2, turn.

Row 24: Color D, dc third st from hook, 3 dc, 5 sc, *5 dc, 5 sc* repeat 3 more times, ch 2, turn.

Row 25: Color A, dc third st from hook, 3 dc, 5 sc, *5 dc, 5 sc* repeat 3 more times, ch 1, turn.

Row 26: Color A, sc second st from hook, 3 sc, 5 dc, *5 sc, 5 dc* repeat 3 more times, ch 1, turn.

Row 27: Color B, sc second st from hook, 3 sc, 5 dc, *5 sc, 5 dc* repeat 3 more times, ch 2, turn.

Row 28: Color B, dc third st from hook, 3 dc, 5 sc, *5 dc, 5 sc* repeat 3 more times, ch 2, turn.

Row 29: Color C, dc third st from hook, 3 dc, 5 sc, *5 dc, 5 sc* repeat 3 more times, ch 1, turn.

Row 30: Color C, sc second st from hook, 3 sc, 5 dc, *5 sc, 5 dc* repeat 3 more times, ch 1, turn.

Row 31: Color A, sc second st from hook, 3 sc, 5 dc, *5 sc, 5 dc* repeat 3 more times, ch 2, turn.

Row 32: Color A, dc third st from hook, 3 dc, 5 sc, *5 dc, 5 sc* repeat 3 more times, ch 2, turn.

Row 33: Color B, dc third st from hook, 3 dc, 5 sc, *5 dc, 5 sc* repeat 3 more times, ch 1, turn.

Row 34: Color B, sc second st from hook, 3 sc, 5 dc, *5 sc, 5 dc* repeat 3 more times, ch 1, turn.

Row 35: Color D, sc second st from hook, 3 sc, 5 dc, *5 sc, 5 dc* repeat 3 more times, ch 2, turn.

Row 36: Color D, dc third st from hook, 3 dc, 5 sc, *5 dc, 5 sc* repeat 3 more times, ch 2, turn.

Row 37: Color A, dc third st from hook, 3 dc, 5 sc, *5 dc, 5 sc* repeat 3 more times, ch 1, turn.

Row 38: Color A, sc second st from hook, 3 sc, 5 dc, *5 sc, 5 dc* repeat 3 more times, ch 1, turn.

Continue for FRONT, LEFT (or skip to BACK instructions rows 33–43)

Row 39: Color B, dc third st from hook, 3 dc, *5 sc, 5 dc* repeat 1 more time ch 2, turn.

Row 40: Color B, dc third st from hook, 3 dc, *5 sc, 5 dc* repeat 1 more time, ch 1, turn.

Row 41: Color D, sc second st from hook, 3 sc, *5 dc, 5 sc* repeat 1 more time, ch 1, turn.

Row 42: Color D, sc 2nd from hook, 3 sc, *5 dc, 5 sc* repeat 1 more time, ch 2, turn.

Row 43: Color A, dc third st from hook, 3 dc, *5 sc, 5 dc* repeat 1 more time, ch 2, turn.

Row 44: Color A, dc third st from hook, 3 dc, *5 sc, 5 dc* ch 1, turn.

Row 45: Color B, sc second st from hook, 3 sc, *5 dc, 5 sc* repeat 1 more time, ch 1, turn.

Row 46: Color B, sc second st from hook, 3 sc, *5 dc, 5 sc* repeat 1 more time, ch 2, turn.

Row 47: Color C, dc third st from hook, 3 dc, *sc, 5 dc* repeat 1 more time, ch 2, turn.

Row 48: Color C, dc third st from hook, 3 dc *5 sc, 5 dc* repeat 1 more time, ch 1, turn.

Row 49: Color B, sc second st from hook, 3 sc, 5 dc.

For FRONT, Right (Picture 1)

Row 39: Color B, sc second st from hook, 3 sc, *5 dc, 5 sc* repeat 1 more time, ch 1, turn.

Row 40: Color B, sc second st from hook, 3 sc, *5 dc, 5 sc* repeat 1 more time, ch 2, turn.

Row 41: Color D, dc third st from hook, 3 dc, *5 sc, 5 dc* repeat 1 more time, ch 2, turn.

Row 42: Color D, dc third st from hook, 3 dc, *5 sc, 5 dc* repeat 1 more time, ch 1, turn.

Row 43: Color A, sc second st from hook, 3 sc, *5 dc, 5 sc* repeat 1 more time ch 1, turn.

Row 44: Color A, sc third st from hook, 3 sc, *5 dc, 5 sc* repeat 1 more time, ch 2, turn.

Row 45: Color B, dc third st from hook, 3 dc, *5 sc, 5 dc* repeat 1 more time, ch 2, turn.

Row 46: Color B, dc third st from hook, 3 dc, *5 sc, 5 dc* repeat 1 more time, ch 1, turn.

Row 47: Color C, sc second st from hook, 3 sc, *5 dc, 5 sc* repeat 1 more time, ch 2, turn.

Row 48: Color C, sc second st from hook, 3 sc, *5 dc, 5 sc* repeat 1 more time, ch 2, turn.

Row 49: Color B, dc third st from hook, 3 dc, 5 sc.
F/O.

BACK

Row 33: Color B, dc third st from hook, 3 dc, 5 sc, *5 dc, 5 sc* repeat 3 more times, ch 1, turn.

Row 34: Color B, sc second st from hook, 3 sc, 5 dc, *5 sc, 5 dc* repeat 3 more times,ch 1, turn.

Row 35: Color D, sc second st from hook, 3 sc, 5 dc, *5 sc, 5 dc*repeat 3 more times, ch 2, turn.

Row 36: Color D, dc third st from hook, 3 dc, 5 sc, *5 dc, 5 sc* repeat 3 more times, ch 2, turn.

Row 37: Color A, dc third st from hook, 3 dc, 5 sc, *5 dc, 5 sc* repeat 3 more times, ch 1, turn.

Row 38: Color A, sc second st from hook, 3 sc, 5 dc, *5 sc, 5 dc* repeat 3

Row 39: Color B, sc second st from hook, 3 sc, 5 dc, *5 sc, 5 dc* repeat 3 more times, ch 2, turn.

Row 40: Color B, dc third st from hook, 3 dc, 5 sc, *5 dc, 5 sc* repeat 3 more times, ch 2, turn.

Row 41: Color C, dc third st from hook, 3 dc, 5 sc, *5 dc, 5 sc* repeat 3 more times, ch 1, turn.

Row 42: Color C, sc second st from hook, 3 sc, 5 dc, *5 sc, 5 dc* repeat 3 more times, ch 1, turn.

Row 43: Color A, sc second st from hook, 3 sc, 5 dc, *5 sc, 5 dc* repeat 3 more times, ch 2, turn.

Row 44: Color A, dc third st from hook, 3 dc, 5 sc, *5 dc, 5 sc* repeat 3 more times, ch 2, turn.

Row 45: Color B, dc third st from hook, 3 dc, 5 sc, *5 dc, 5 sc* repeat 3 more times, ch 1, turn.

Row 46: Color B, sc second st from hook, 3 sc, 5 dc, *5 sc, 5 dc* repeat 3 more times, ch 1, turn.

Row 47: Color D, sc second st from hook, 3 sc, 5 dc, *5 sc, 5 dc* repeat 3 more times, ch 2, turn.

Row 48: Color D, dc third st from hook, 3 dc, 5 sc, *5 dc, 5 sc* repeat 3 more times, ch 2, turn.

Row 49: Color A, dc third st from hook, 3 dc, 5 sc, *5 dc, 5 sc* repeat 3 more times, ch 1, turn.

Row 50: Color A, sc second st from hook, 3 sc, 5 dc, *5 sc, 5 dc* repeat 3 more times, ch 2, turn.
Stitch front and back together, leaving 5½" opening for sleeve.

SLEEVE (Picture 2)

Round 1: Color D, sl st, ch 1, 39 dc around.
Round 2: Color D, dc dec, 38 dc around.
Round 3: Color D, dc dec, 37 dc around.
Round 4: Color D, dc dec, 36 dc around.
Round 5: Color D, dc dec, 35 dc around.
Round 6: Color D, dc dec, 44 dc around.
Rounds 7–15: Color D, 45 dc around.
Rounds 16–17: Color D, *7 sc, 7 dc*

repeat 2 more times.
Rounds 18–19: Color B, *7 dc, 7 sc* repeat 2 more times.
Rounds 20–21: Color A, *7 sc, 7 dc* repeat 2 more times.
Round 22: Color C, *7 dc, 7 sc* repeat 2 more times.
Round 23: Color C, *7 dc, 7 sc* repeat 2 more times.

HOOD (Picture 3)

Row 1: Color D, sl st to collar, ch 2, 55 dc across, ch 2, turn.
Rows 2–23: 56 dc across, ch 2, turn.
Row 24: 56 dc across.
F/O.
Fold and stitch top of hood together.

SIZE AGE 6
FRONT AND BACK

Color A, ch 61.

Row 1: Color A, dc third st from hook, 3 dc, 5 sc, *5 dc, 5 sc* repeat 4 more times, ch 1, turn.

Row 2: Color A, sc second st from hook, 3 sc, 5 dc, *5 sc, 5 dc* repeat 2 more times, ch 1, turn.

Row 3: Color B, sc second st from hook, 3 sc, 5 dc, *5 sc, 5 dc* repeat 2 more times, ch 2, turn.

Row 4: Color B, dc third st from hook, 3 sc, 5 dc, *5 sc, 5 dc* repeat 2 more times, ch 2, turn.

Row 5: Color C, dc third st from hook, 3 dc, 5 sc, *5 dc, 5 sc* repeat 2 more times, ch 1, turn.

Row 6: Color C, sc second st from hook, 3 sc, 5 dc, *5 sc, 5 dc* repeat 2 more times, ch 1, turn.

Row 7: Color A, sc second st from hook, 3 sc, 5 dc, *5 sc, 5 dc* repeat 2 more times, ch 2, turn.

Row 8: Color A, dc third st from hook, 3 dc, 5 sc, *5 dc, 5 sc* repeat 2 more times, ch 2, turn.

Row 9: Color B, dc third st from hook, 3 dc, 5 sc, *5 dc, 5 sc* repeat 2 more times, ch 1, turn.

Row 10: Color B, sc second st from hook, 3 sc, 5 dc, *5 sc, 5 dc* repeat 2 more times, ch 1, turn.

Row 11: Color D, sc second st from hook, 3 sc, 5 dc, *5 sc, 5 dc* repeat 2 more times, ch 2, turn.

Row 12: Color D, dc third st from hook, 3 dc, 5 sc, *5 dc, 5 sc* repeat 2 more times, ch 2, turn.

Row 13: Color A, dc third st from hook, 3 dc, 5 sc, *5 dc, 5 sc* repeat 2 more times, ch 1, turn.

Row 14: Color A, sc second st from hook, 3 sc, 5 dc, *5 sc, 5 dc* repeat 2 more times, ch 1, turn.

Row 15: Color B, sc second st from hook, 3 sc, 5 dc, *5 sc, 5 dc* repeat 2 more times, ch 2, turn.

Row 16: Color B, dc third st from hook, 3 dc, 5 sc, *5 dc, 5 sc* repeat 2 more times, ch 2, turn.

Row 17: Color C, dc third st from hook, 3 dc, 5 sc, *5 dc, 5 sc* repeat 2 more times, ch 1, turn.

Row 18: Color C, sc second st from hook, 3 sc, 5 dc, *5 sc, 5 dc* repeat 2 more times, ch 1, turn.

Row 19: Color A, sc second st from hook, 3 sc, 5 dc, *5 sc, 5 dc* repeat 2 more times, ch 2, turn.

Row 20: Color A, dc third st from hook, 3 dc, 5 sc, *5 dc, 5 sc* repeat 2 more times, ch 2, turn.

Row 21: Color B, dc third st from hook, 3 dc, 5 sc, *5 dc, 5 sc* repeat 2 more times, ch 1, turn.

Row 22: Color B, sc second st from hook, 3 sc, 5 dc, *5 sc, 5 dc* repeat 2 more times, ch 1, turn.

Row 23: Color D, sc second st from hook, 3 sc, 5 dc, *5 sc, 5 dc* repeat 2 more times, ch 2, turn.

Row 24: Color D, dc third st from hook, 3 dc, 5 sc, *5 dc, 5 sc* repeat 2 more times, ch 2, turn.

Row 25: Color A, dc third st from hook, 3 dc, 5 sc, *5 dc, 5 sc* repeat 2 more times, ch 1, turn.

Row 26: Color A, sc second st from hook, 3 sc, 5 dc, *5 sc, 5 dc* repeat 2 more times, ch 1, turn.

Row 27: Color B, sc second st from hook, 3 sc, 5 dc, *5 sc, 5 dc* repeat 2 more times, ch 2, turn.

Row 28: Color B, dc third st from hook, 3 dc, 5 sc, *5 dc, 5 sc* repeat 2 more times, ch 2, turn.

Row 29: Color C, dc third st from hook, 3 dc, 5 sc, *5 dc, 5 sc* repeat 2 more times, ch 1, turn.

Row 30: Color C, sc second st from hook, 3 sc, 5 dc, *5 sc, 5 dc* repeat 2 more times, ch 1, turn.

Row 31: Color A, sc second st from hook, 3 sc, 5 dc, *5 sc, 5 dc* repeat 2 more times, ch 2, turn.

Row 32: Color A, dc third st from hook, 3 dc, 5 sc, *5 dc, 5 sc* repeat 2 more times, ch 2, turn.

Row 33: Color B, dc third st from hook, 3 dc, 5 sc, *5 dc, 5 sc* repeat 2 more times, ch 1, turn.

Row 34: Color B, sc second st from hook, 3 sc, 5 dc, *5 sc, 5 dc* repeat 2 more times, ch 1, turn.

Row 35: Color D, sc second st from hook, 3 sc, 5 dc, *5 sc, 5 dc* repeat 2 more times, ch 2, turn.

Row 36: Color D, dc third st from hook, 3 dc, 5 sc, *5 dc, 5 sc* repeat 2 more times, ch 2, turn.

Row 37: Color A, dc third st from hook, 3 dc, 5 sc, *5 dc, 5 sc* repeat 2 more times, ch 1, turn.

Row 38: Color A, sc second st from hook, 3 sc, 5 dc, *5 sc, 5 dc* repeat 2 more times, ch 1, turn.

Row 39: Color B, sc second st from hook, 3 sc, 5 dc, *5 sc, 5 dc* repeat 2 more times, ch 2, turn.

Row 40: Color B, dc third st from hook, 3 dc, 5 sc, *5 dc, 5 sc* repeat 2 more times, ch 2, turn.

Row 41: Color C, dc third st from hook, 3 dc, 5 sc, *5 dc, 5 sc* repeat 2 more times, ch 1, turn.

Row 42: Color C, sc second st from hook, 3 sc, 5 dc, *5 sc, 5 dc* repeat 2 more times, ch 1, turn.

Row 43: Color A, sc second st from hook, 3 sc, 5 dc, *5 sc, 5 dc* repeat 2 more times, ch 2, turn.

Row 44: Color A, dc third st from hook, 3 dc, 5 sc, *5 dc, 5 sc* repeat 2 more times, ch 2, turn.

Continue for FRONT, LEFT (or skip to BACK instructions rows 33–43).

Row 45: Color B, dc third st from hook, 3 dc, 5 sc, 5 dc, 5 sc, ch 1, turn.

Row 46: Color B, sc second st from hook, 3 sc, 5 dc, 5 sc, 5 dc, ch 1, turn.

Row 47: Color D, sc second st from hook, 3 sc, 5 dc, 5 sc, 5 dc, ch 2, turn.

Row 48: Color D, dc third st from hook, 3 dc, 5 sc, 5 dc, 5 sc, ch 2, turn.

Row 49: Color A, dc third st from hook, 3 dc, 5 sc, 5 dc, 5 sc, ch 1, turn.

Row 50: Color A, sc second st from hook, 3 sc, 5 dc, 5 sc, 5 dc, ch 1, turn.

Row 51: Color B, sc second st from hook, 3 sc, 5 dc, 5 sc, 5 dc, ch 2, turn.

Row 52: Color B, dc third st from hook, 3 dc, 5 sc, 5 dc, 5 sc, ch 2, turn.

Row 53: Color C, dc third st from hook, 3 dc, 5 sc, 5 dc, 5 sc, ch 1, turn.

Row 54: Color C, sc second st from hook, 3 sc, 5 dc, 5 sc, 5 dc, ch 1, turn.

Row 55: Color B, sc second st from hook, 3 sc, 5 dc.

For FRONT, Right (Picture 1)

Row 45: Color B, sc third st from hook, 3 sc, 5 dc, 5 sc, 5 dc, ch 2, turn.

Row 46: Color B, dc second st from hook, 3 dc, 5 sc, 5 dc, 5 sc, ch 2, turn.

Row 47: Color D, dc second st from hook, 3 dc, 5 sc, 5 dc, 5 sc, ch 1, turn.

Row 48: Color D, sc third st from hook, 3 sc, 5 dc, 5 sc, 5 dc, ch 1, turn.

Row 49: Color A, sc third st from hook, 3 sc, 5 dc, 5 sc, 5 dc, ch 2, turn.

Row 50: Color A, dc second st from hook, 3 dc, 5 sc, 5 dc, 5 sc, ch 2, turn.

Row 51: Color B, dc second st from hook, 3 dc, 5 sc, 5 dc, 5 sc, ch 1, turn.

Row 52: Color B, sc third st from hook, 3 sc, 5 dc, 5 sc, 5 dc, ch 1, turn.

Row 53: Color C, sc third st from hook, 3 sc, 5 dc, 5 sc, 5 dc, ch 2, turn.

Row 54: Color C, dc second st from hook, 3 dc, 5 sc, 5 dc, 5 sc, ch 2, turn.

Row 55: Color B, dc second st from hook, 3 dc, 5 sc.
F/O.

BACK

Row 45: Color B, dc third st from hook, 3 dc, 5 sc, *5 dc, 5 sc* repeat 2 more times, ch 1, turn.
Row 46: Color B, sc second st from hook, 3 sc, 5 dc, *5 sc, 5 dc* repeat 2 more times, ch 1, turn.
Row 47: Color D, sc second st from hook, 3 sc, 5 dc, *5 sc, 5 dc* repeat 2 more times, ch 2, turn.
Row 48: Color D, dc third st from hook, 3 dc, 5 sc, *5 dc, 5 sc* repeat 2 more times, ch 2, turn.
Row 49: Color A, dc third st from hook, 3 dc, 5 sc, *5 dc, 5 sc* repeat 2 more times, ch 1, turn.
Row 50: Color A, sc second st from hook, 3 sc, 5 dc, *5 sc, 5 dc* repeat 2 more times, ch 1, turn.
Row 51: Color B, sc second st from hook, 3 sc, 5 dc, *5 sc, 5 dc* repeat 2 more times, ch 2, turn.
Row 52: Color B, dc third st from hook, 3 dc, 5 sc, *5 dc, 5 sc* repeat 2 more times, ch 2, turn.
Row 53: Color C, dc third st from hook, 3 dc, 5 sc, *5 dc, 5 sc* repeat 2 more times, ch 1, turn.
Row 54: Color C, sc second st from hook, 3 sc, 5 dc, *5 sc, 5 dc* repeat 2 more times, ch 1, turn.
Row 55: Color A, sc second st from hook, 3 sc, 5 dc, *5 sc, 5 dc* repeat 2 more times, ch 2, turn.
Stitch front and back together, leaving 6" opening for sleeve.

SLEEVE (Picture 2)

Round 1: Color D, sl st, ch 1, 49 dc around.
Round 2: Color D, dc dec, 48 dc around.
Round 3: Color D, dc dec, 47 dc around.
Round 4: Color D, dc dec, 46 dc around.
Round 5: Color D, dc dec, 45 dc around.
Round 6: Color D, dc dec, 44 dc around.
Rounds 7–21: Color D, 45 dc around.

Rounds 22–23: Color D, *7 sc, 7 dc* repeat 2 more times.
Rounds 24–25: Color B, *7 dc, 7 sc* repeat 2 more times.
Rounds 26–27: Color A, *7 sc, 7 dc* repeat 2 more times.
Round 28: Color C, *7 dc, 7 sc* repeat 2 more times.
Round 29: Color C, *7 sc, 7 dc* repeat 2 more times.

HOOD (Picture 3)

Row 1: Color D, sl st to collar, ch 2, 55 dc across, ch 2, turn.
Rows 2–25: 56 dc across, ch 2, turn.
Row 26: 56 dc across.
F/O.
Fold and stitch top of hood together.

Robot Vest

My children love robots! Doesn't everyone? There is a cute pocket on the front for little toys and a fun robot peeking out. The basket weave design on this vest adds texture to the design. The simple vest without appliqués would also be perfect for the holidays, a wedding party, or any fancy affair.

Materials

- Cascade Ultra Pima 10 x 100g/220yds 100% Pima Cotton
  - Color #3798 / color name Suede / 2 skeins
- Small amounts of Ultra Pima for robot:
  - Color #3713 / color name Wine, #3754 / color name True Black
  - Color #3739 / color name Lime, #3732 / color name Aqua
  - Color #3728 / color name White
- 4 buttons
- **Hooks:** H (5mm) for vest and G (4mm) for robot

Skill level: Advanced

Gauge: 8 sc=2", 8 sc rows = 2"

Glossary of abbreviations

ch – chain
sc – single crochet
dc – double crochet
sl st – slip stitch
sk – skip
FPDC – Front Post double crochet
BPDC – Back Post double crochet
F/O – fasten off
(#) number of stitches at end of round
* _ * to be repeated (repeat)

Helpful Tips – At end of each row, skip last post.
Front Post double crochet: double crochet from the front side of the post.
Back Post double crochet: double crochet from the backside of the post.

SIZE AGES 1/2
BACK
Ch 41.
Row 1: dc second st from hook and across, ch 2, turn.
Rows 2–5: *4FPDC, 4 BPDC* repeat 4 more times, ch 2, turn.
Rows 6–9: *4BPDC, 4 FPDC* repeat 4 more times, ch 2, turn.
Rows 10–13: *4FPDC, 4 BPDC* repeat 4 more times, ch 2, turn.
Rows 14–17: *4BPDC, 4 FPDC* repeat 4 more times, ch 2, turn.
Rows 18–21: *4FPDC, 4 BPDC* repeat 4 more times, ch 2, turn.

Rows 22–24: *4BPDC, 4 FPDC* repeat 4 more times, ch 2, turn.
Row 25: *4BPDC, 4 FPDC* repeat 4 more times, (do not ch 2), turn.
Row 26: 4 sl st, *4BPDC, 4 FPDC* repeat 3 more times, ch 2, turn (leave last 4 sts unworked).
Rows 27–29: *4BPDC, 4 FPDC* repeat 3 more times, ch 2, turn.
Rows 30–33: *4FPDC, 4 BPDC* repeat 3 more times, ch 2, turn.
Rows 34–37: *4BPDC, 4 FPDC* repeat 3 more times, ch 2, turn.
F/O.

FRONT (Make 2)
Ch 25.
Row 1: dc in second st from hook and across, ch 2, turn.
Rows 2–5: *4FPDC, 4 BPDC* repeat 2 more times, ch 2, turn.
Rows 6–9: *4BPDC, 4 FPDC* repeat 2 more times, ch 2, turn.
Rows 10–13: *4FPDC, 4 BPDC* repeat 2 more times, ch 2, turn.
Rows 14–17: *4BPDC, 4 FPDC* repeat 2 more times, ch 2, turn.
Rows 18–21: *4FPDC, 4 BPDC* repeat 2 more times, ch 2, turn.
Rows 22–24: *4BPDC, 4 FPDC* repeat

Picture 1: Yarn over.

Picture 2: Insert hook under post of next stitch.

Picture 3: Yarn over.

2 more times, ch 2, turn.

Row 25: *4BPDC, 4 FPDC* repeat 2 more times, (No ch 2), turn.

Row 26: 4 sl st, *4BPDC, 4 FPDC* repeat 1 more time, 4 BPDC, ch 2, turn (leave last 4 sts unworked).

Row 27: *4FPDC, 4BPDC* repeat 1 more time, 4FPDC, ch 2, turn.

Row 28: *4BPDC, 4FPDC* repeat 1 more time, 4BPDC, ch 2, turn.

Rows 29: *4FPDC, 4BPDC* repeat 1 more time, 4FPDC, ch 2, turn.

Row 30: 4FPDC, 4BPDC, 4FPDC, ch 2, turn.

Row 31: 4BPDC, 4FPDC, 4BPDC, ch 2, turn.

Row 32: 4FPDC, 4BPDC, 4FPDC, ch 2, turn.

Row 33: 4BPDC, 4FPDC, 4BPDC, ch 2, turn.

Row 34–38: 4BPDC, 4FPDC, ch 2, turn. F/O.

SIZE AGES 3/4
BACK

Ch 49.

Row 1: dc second st from hook and across, ch 2, turn.

Rows 2–5: *4FPDC, 4 BPDC* repeat 5 more times, ch 2, turn.

Rows 6–9: *4BPDC, 4 FPDC* repeat 5 more times, ch 2, turn.

Rows 10–13: *4FPDC, 4 BPDC* repeat 5 more times, ch 2, turn.

Rows 14–17: *4FPDC, 4 FPDC* repeat 5 more times, ch 2, turn.

Rows 18–21: *4FPDC, 4 BPDC* repeat 5 more times, ch 2, turn.

Rows 22–25: *4BPDC, 4 FPDC* repeat 5 more times, ch 2, turn.

Rows 26–29: *4FPDC, 4 BPDC* repeat 5 more times, ch 2, turn.

Rows 30–32: *4BPDC, 4 FPDC* repeat 5 more times, ch 2, turn.

Row 33: *4BPDC, 4 FPDC* repeat 5 more times, (do not ch 2), turn.

Row 34: 4 sl st, *4BPDC, 4 FPDC* repeat 4 more times, ch 2, turn (leave last 4 sts unworked).

Rows 35–37: *4BPDC, 4 FPDC* repeat

3 more times, ch 2, turn.

Rows 38–41: *4FPDC, 4 BPDC* repeat 3 more times, ch 2, turn.

Rows 42–45: *4BPDC, 4 FPDC* repeat 3 more times, ch 2, turn.

F/O.

FRONT (Make 2)

Ch 29.

Row 1: dc in second st from hook and across, ch 2, turn.

Row 2: *4FPDC, 4BPDC* repeat 2 more times, 4 FPDC, ch 2, turn.

Row 3: *4BPDC, 4FPDC* repeat 2 more times, 4 BPDC, ch 2, turn.

Row 4: *4FPDC, 4BPDC* repeat 2 more times, 4 FPDC, ch 2, turn.

Row 5: *4BPDC, 4FPDC* repeat 2 more times, 4 BPDC, ch 2, turn.

Row 6: *4BPDC, 4FPDC* repeat 2 more times, 4 BPDC, ch 2, turn.

Row 7: *4FPDC, 4BPDC* repeat 2 more times, 4 FPDC, ch 2, turn.

Row 8: *4BPDC, 4FPDC* repeat 2 more times, 4 BPDC, ch 2, turn.

Row 9: *4FPDC, 4BPDC* repeat 2 more times, 4 FPDC, ch 2, turn.

Row 10: *4FPDC, 4BPDC* repeat 2 more times, 4 FPDC, ch 2, turn.

Row 11: *4BPDC, 4FPDC* repeat 2 more times, 4 BPDC, ch 2, turn.

Row 12: *4FPDC, 4BPDC* repeat 2 more times, 4 FPDC, ch 2, turn.

Row 13: *4BPDC, 4FPDC* repeat 2 more times, 4 BPDC, ch 2, turn.

Row 14: *4BPDC, 4FPDC* repeat 2 more times, 4 BPDC, ch 2, turn.

Row 15: *4FPDC, 4BPDC* repeat 2 more times, 4 FPDC, ch 2, turn.

Row 16: *4BPDC, 4FPDC* repeat 2 more times, 4 BPDC, ch 2, turn.

Row 17: *4FPDC, 4BPDC* repeat 2 more times, 4 FPDC, ch 2, turn.

Row 18: *4FPDC, 4BPDC* repeat 2 more times, 4 FPDC, ch 2, turn.

Row 19: *4BPDC, 4FPDC* repeat 2 more times, 4 BPDC, ch 2, turn.

Row 20: *4FPDC, 4BPDC* repeat 2 more times, 4 FPDC, ch 2, turn.

Row 21: *4BPDC, 4FPDC* repeat 2

Picture 4: Pull through post.

Picture 5: Yarn over.

Picture 6: Pull through all loops on hook.

more times, 4 BPDC, ch 2, turn.
Row 22: *4BPDC, 4FPDC* repeat 2 more times, 4 BPDC, ch 2, turn.
Row 23: *4FPDC, 4BPDC* repeat 2 more times, 4 FPDC, ch 2, turn.
Row 24: *4BPDC, 4FPDC* repeat 2 more times, 4 BPDC, ch 2, turn.
Row 25: *4FPDC, 4BPDC* repeat 2 more times, 4 FPDC, ch 2, turn.
Row 26: *4FPDC, 4BPDC* repeat 2 more times, 4 FPDC, ch 2, turn.
Row 27: *4BPDC, 4FPDC* repeat 2 more times, 4 BPDC, ch 2, turn.
Row 28: *4FPDC, 4BPDC* repeat 2 more times, 4 FPDC, ch 2, turn.
Row 29: *4BPDC, 4FPDC* repeat 2 more times, 4 BPDC, ch 2, turn.
Row 30: *4BPDC, 4FPDC* repeat 2 more times, 4 BPDC, ch 2, turn.
Row 31: *4FPDC, 4BPDC* repeat 2 more times, 4 FPDC, ch 2, turn.
Row 32: *4BPDC, 4FPDC* repeat 2 more times, 4 BPDC, ch 2, turn.
Row 33: *4FPDC, 4BPDC* repeat 2 more times, 4 FPDC, (do not ch 2), turn.
Row: 34: *4FPDC, 4BPDC* repeat 2 more times, ch 2, turn, (leave last sts unworked).
Rows 35–37: *4FPDC, 4BPDC* repeat 2 more times, ch 2, turn, (leave last sts unworked).
Rows 38–41: *4BPDC, 4FPDC* repeat 1 more time, ch 2, turn.
Rows 42–44: 4FPDC, 4BPDC, 4FPDC, ch 2, turn.
Row 45: 4FPDC, 4BPDC, 4FPDC.
F/O.

ROBOT PIECES

Body
With Red, ch 20.
Rows 1–25: sc second st from hook and across, ch 1, turn.
F/O.

Head
With Red, ch 15.
Rows 1–17: sc second st from hook and across, ch 1, turn.
With Black – 8 dc across middle/top of head.

Eyes
With Black – ch 2, 6 sc second st from hook.
With White – 2 sc in each around. (12)
With Blue – 2 sc in first, sc next st, *2 sc, 1 sc* repeat for 18 total.
F/O.

Hands/Feet
Ch 6, dc second st from hook, 3 dc next st, 3 dc next st, dc, ch 2, sl st last.
F/O.

Front Pocket
Ch 20.
Rows 1–20: sc second st from hook and across, ch 1, turn.
F/O.

Spring Tunic Dress

2-6 years

I love Spring. Flowers are blooming, grass is turning green, and the weather is perfect. This dress combines two of my favorite things: granny squares and chevrons.

Materials

- Cascade Pima Silk 10 x 50g/109 yds 85% Peruvian Pima Cotton 15% Silk
  – Color #0638 / color name Lilac / 5 skeins (Color A)
  – Color #6915 / color name China Pink / 1 skein (Color B)
  – Color #9678 / color name Water Lily Red / 1 skein (Color C)
- **Hooks:** G (4mm) for squares and skirt of size ages 2/3 and H (5mm) for skirt of size ages 4/5 and 6

Skill level: Intermediate

Gauge: Size 5mm hook, 8 sc = 2", 8 sc rows = 2"

Glossary of abbreviations

ch – chain
sc – single crochet
dc – double crochet
hdc – half double crochet
sl st – slip stitch
sk – skip
sp – space
Cluster: (2 next to each other look like a heart) *y/o, insert hook in indicated st and pull up a loop, y/o and pull through 2 loops* repeat 4 times, y/o and pull through all 5 remaining loops on hook.
F/O – fasten off
y/o – yarn over
{ _ } numerous stitches to be repeated in one space
* _ * to be repeated
Round – continues in a circle
Row – goes back and forth

SQUARES (Make 7) SIZE AGES 2/3
Color A.
Round 1: ch 2, 4 sc in second st from hook.
Round 2: sl st to top of first sc, ch 1, sc same, ch 1, *2 sc next st, ch 1* repeat 2 more times.
Color B.
Round 3: sl st to ch 1 sp, *{Cluster, ch 2, Cluster} all in ch 1 space, ch 1* repeat 3 more times around. (Total of four – 2 cluster groups that look like hearts.)
Color C.
Round 4: sl st to ch 2 {Ch 1, 2 sc, ch 1, 3 sc} all in middle of cluster heart, 3 sc in next ch 2 space, *{3 sc, ch 1, 3 sc} all in middle of cluster heart, 3 sc in next ch 2 space* repeat 2 more times.
Color A.
Round 5: 2 sc, *{sc, ch 1, sc} in corner, sc in each of next 9 sts* repeat 2 more times, {sc, ch 1, sc} in corner, sc in each of next 7 sts. F/O.
Sew squares together. (Picture 2)

Sew middle squares together. (Picture 3)

SIZE AGES 2/3
Use size G, (4mm) hook.
Color A
Round 1: Sl St to one st to side of corner peak, (Picture 4), Ch 2, 10 Dc, Sk 2 (at corner of square), 11 Dc, 3 Dc in next st (at corner peak), *11 Dc, Sk 2, 11 Dc, 3 Dc next* repeat 4 more times
Round 2: *11 Dc, Sk 2, 11 Dc, 3 Dc next* repeat 5 more times
Round 3: *11 Dc, Sk 2, 11 Dc, 3 Dc next* repeat 5 more times
Color B
Round 4: *11 Sc, Sk 2, 11 Sc, 3 Sc next*, repeat 5 more times
Color A
Round 5-7: *11 Dc, Sk 2, 11 Dc, 3 Dc next* repeat 5 more times
Color C
Round 8: *11 Sc, Sk 2, 11 Sc, 3 Sc next*, repeat 5 more times

Color A
Round 9-11: *11 Dc, Sk 2, 11 Dc, 3 Dc next* repeat 5 more times
Color B
Round 4: *11 Sc, Sk 2, 11 Sc, 3 Sc next*, repeat 5 more times.
Color A
Round 5-7: *11 Dc, Sk 2, 11 Dc, 3 Dc next* repeat 5 more times.
Color C
Round 8: *11 Sc, Sk 2, 11 Sc, 3 Sc next*, repeat 5 more times.
Color A

Picture 1: 3" x 3" square for sizes ages 4-6. 2 ½" x 2 ½" square for sizes ages 2/3.

Picture 2: Attach squares as indicated.

Round 9-11: *11 Dc, Sk 2, 11 Dc, 3 Dc next* repeat 5 more times.
Color B
Round 12: *11 Sc, Sk 2, 11 Sc, 3 Sc next*, repeat 5 more times.
Color A
Round 13-15: *11 Dc, Sk 2, 11 Dc, 3 Dc next* repeat 5 more times.
Color C
Round 16: *11 Sc, Sk 2, 11 Sc, 3 Sc next*, repeat 5 more times.
Color A
Round 17-19: *11 Dc, Sk 2, 11 Dc, 3 Dc next* repeat 5 more times.
Color B
Round 20: *11 Sc, Sk 2, 11 Sc, 3 Sc next*, repeat 5 more times.
Color A
Round 21-23: *11 Dc, Sk 2, 11 Dc, 3 Dc next* repeat 5 more times.
Color C
Round 24: *11 Sc, Sk 2, 11 Sc, 3 Sc next*, repeat 5 more times.

SQUARES (Make 7) SIZE 4/5 AND 6

Color A.
Round 1: ch 2, 4 sc in second st from hook.
Round 2: sl st to top of first sc, ch 2, dc same, ch 1, *2 dc next st, ch 1* repeat 2 more times.
Color B.
Round 3: sl st to ch 1 sp, *{Cluster, ch 2, Cluster} all in ch 1 space, ch 1* repeat 3 more times around. (Total of four 2 cluster groups that look like hearts.)
Color C.
Round 4: sl st to ch 1 {Ch 2, 2 dc, ch 1, 3 dc} all in middle of cluster heart, 3 dc in next ch 2 space, *{3 dc, ch 1, 3 dc} all in middle of cluster heart, 3 dc in next ch 2 space* repeat 2 more times.
Color A.
Round 5: 2 sc, *{sc, ch 1, sc} in corner, sc in each of next 9 sts* repeat 2 more times, {sc, ch 1, sc} in corner, sc in each of next 7 sts. F/O.
Sew squares together. (Picture 2)
For size 4/5: sew two middle squares together (Picture 3)

SIZE AGES 4/5
Use size H, (5mm) hook.

Color A.
Round 1: sl st to one st to side of corner peak, (Picture 4), ch 2, 10 dc, sk 2 (at corner of square), 11 dc, 3 dc in next st (at corner peak), *11 dc, sk 2, 11 dc, 3 dc next st* repeat 4 more times.

Round 2: *11 dc, sk 2, 11 dc, 3 dc next st* repeat 5 more times.

Round 3: *11 dc, sk 2, 11 dc, 3 dc next st* repeat 5 more times.

Color B.
Round 4: *11 sc, sk 2, 11 sc, 3 sc next st* repeat 5 more times.

Color A.
Round 5–7: *11 dc, sk 2, 11 dc, 3 dc next st* repeat 5 more times.

Color C.
Round 8: *11 sc, sk 2, 11 sc, 3 sc next st* repeat 5 more times.

Color A.
Round 9–11: *11 dc, sk 2, 11 dc, 3 dc next st* repeat 5 more times.

Color B.
Round 4: *11 sc, sk 2, 11 sc, 3 sc next st* repeat 5 more times.

Color A.
Round 5–7: *11 dc, sk 2, 11 dc, 3 dc next st* repeat 5 more times.

Color C.
Round 8: *11 sc, sk 2, 11 sc, 3 sc next st* repeat 5 more times.

Color A.
Round 9–11: *11 dc, sk 2, 11 dc, 3 dc next st* repeat 5 more times.

Color B.
Round 12: *11 sc, sk 2, 11 sc, 3 sc next st* repeat 5 more times.

Color A.
Round 13–15: *11 dc, sk 2, 11 dc, 3 dc next st* repeat 5 more times.

Color C.
Round 16: *11 sc, sk 2, 11 sc, 3 sc next st* repeat 5 more times.

Color A.
Round 17–19: *11 dc, sk 2, 11 dc, 3 dc next st* repeat 5 more times.

Color B.
Round 20: *11 sc, sk 2, 11 sc, 3 sc next

Picture 3: Stitch middle of top together for size ages 2/3 and 4/5 at 'X'.

Picture 4: Starting chevron design from dress top.

st* repeat 5 more times.
Color A.
Round 21–23: *11 dc, sk 2, 11 dc, 3 dc next st* repeat 5 more times.
Color C.
Round 24: *11 sc, sk 2, 11 sc, 3 sc next st* repeat 5 more times.
Color A.
Round 25–27: *11 dc, sk 2, 11 dc, 3 dc next st* repeat 5 more times.
Color B.
Round 28: *11 sc, sk 2, 11 sc, 3 sc next st* repeat 5 more times.
Color A.
Round 29–31: *11 dc, sk 2, 11 dc, 3 dc next st* repeat 5 more times.
Color C.
Round 32: *11 sc, sk 2, 11 sc, 3 sc next st* repeat 5 more times.
Color A.
Round 33–35: *11 dc, sk 2, 11 dc, 3 dc next st* repeat 5 more times.

SIZE AGE 6

Do not stitch middle squares together. (Leave as in Picture 2.)
Repeat all steps 1–35 on Size ages 4/5.
Color B.
Round 36: *11 sc, sk 2, 11 sc, 3 sc next st* repeat 5 more times.
Color A.
Round 37–39: *11 dc, sk 2, 11 dc, 3 dc next st* repeat 5 more times.
Color C.
Round 40: *11 sc, sk 2, 11 sc, 3 sc next st* repeat 5 more times.
Color A.
Round 41–43: *11 dc, sk 2, 11 dc, 3 dc next st* repeat 5 more times. F/O.

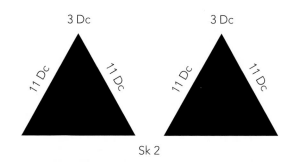

Summer

Daisy Brimmed Hat

If you live in a warm climate, you rarely have an opportunity to wear a winter hat. This cool cotton hat provides shade from the heat of the summer sun. The daisy was added because all little girls love flowers. This hat can also be made for boys to wear on a day of fishing with dad.

Materials

- Cascade Ultra Pima 10 x 100g/220yds 100% Pima Cotton
  – Color #3736 / color name Ice / 2 skeins (Color A)
- Cascade Eco Alpaca 100g/220 yds 100% Natural Undyed Alpaca
  – Color #3718 / color name Natural / 1 skein (Color B)
  – Color #3764 / color name Sunshine / 1 skein (Color C)
- **Hook:** H (5mm)

Skill level: Easy   **Gauge:** 2" Circle at end of round 3 (30 hdc)

Glossary of abbreviations

ch – chain
hdc – half double crochet
sl st – slip stitch
sk – skip,
dtr – double treble crochet –
    Yarn over hook three times,
    then insert hook into next
    stitch. Yarn over hook and
    draw yarn through stitch – five
    loops on the hook. Loop yarn
    over hook and draw through
    two loops, (there are now
    four loops remaining on the
    hook), *yarn over hook and
    draw through two loops*
    repeat *to* 2 more times. This
    completes one double treble
    crochet.
y/o – yarn over
F/O – fasten off
BPSC – back post single crochet
    (single crochet from the
    backside of the post)
BLO – back loop only
(#) number of stitches at end of
    round
* _ * to be repeated
round – continues in a circle

Helpful Tips – BPSC will cause the prior round to "pop out".
Picture 1: Insert hook behind post.
Picture 2: Pull yarn through, yarn over.
Picture 3: Pull all loops through to finish single crochet.
Picture 4: BLO will create a rippled effect around brim.

TODDLER'S SIZE

Round 1: ch 2, 10 hdc in second st from hook. (10)

Round 2: sl st to top of first hdc, ch 1, hdc in same st, 2 hdc in each stitch around. (20)

Round 3: sl st to top of first hdc, ch 1, hdc in same st, hdc in next st, *2 hdc in next st, hdc in next st* repeat around. (30)

Round 4: sl st to top of first hdc, ch 1, hdc in same st, hdc in each of next 2 sts, *2 hdc in next st, hdc in each of next 2 sts* repeat around. (40)

Round 5: sl st to top of first hdc, ch 1, hdc in same st, hdc in each of next 3 sts, *2 hdc in next st, hdc in each of next 3 sts* repeat around. (50)

Round 6: sl st to top of first hdc, ch 1, hdc in same st, hdc in each of next 4 sts, *2 hdc in next st, hdc in each of next 4 sts* repeat around. (60)

Round 7: sl st to top of first hdc, ch 1, hdc in same st, hdc in each of next 8 sts, *2 hdc in next st, hdc in each of next 8 sts* repeat around, hdc in last 6 sts. (66)

Round 8: BLO (this row is to be completed in BLO) sl st to top of first hdc, ch 1, hdc in next st and around. (66)

Round 9: sl st to top of first hdc, ch 1, hdc in next st and around. (66)

Round 10: sl st to top of first hdc, ch 1, hdc in next st and around. (66)

Picture 1: Insert hook behind post.

Picture 2: Yarn over and pull through post.

Round 11: sl st to top of first hdc, ch 1, hdc in next st and around. (66)

Round 12: **Color B this round.** Sl st to top of first hdc, ch 1, hdc in next st and around. (66) Change back to Color A at y/o of last hdc of this round.

Round 13: BPSC around. (66)

Round 14: sl st to top of first hdc, ch 1, hdc in next st and around. (66)

Round 15: sl st to top of first hdc, ch 1, hdc in next st and around. (66)

Round 16: **Color B this round.** Sl st to top of first hdc, ch 1, hdc in next st and around. (66) Change back to Color A at y/o of last hdc of this round.

Round 17: BPSC around. (66)

Round 18: sl st to top of hdc, ch 1, hdc in same st, hdc in each of next 5 sts, *2 hdc in next st, hdc in each of next 5 sts* repeat around, hdc in last 6 sts. (76)

Round 19: BLO, sl st to top of first hdc, ch 1, hdc in next st and around. (76)

Round 20: BLO, sl st to top of first hdc, ch 1, hdc in same st, hdc in each of next 6 sts, *2 hdc in next st, hdc in each of next 6 sts* repeat around, hdc in last 6 sts. (86)

Round 21: BLO, sl st to top of first hdc, ch 1, hdc in next st and around. (86)

Round 22: BLO, sl st to top of first hdc, ch 1, hdc in same st, hdc in each of next 7 sts, *2 hdc in next st, hdc in each of next 7 sts* repeat around, hdc in last 6 sts. (96)

Round 23: BLO, sl st to top of first hdc, ch 1, hdc in next st and around. (96), sl st to next st and F/O (turn right side out).

CHILD'S SIZE

Round 1: ch 2, 10 hdc in second st from hook. (10)

Round 2: sl st to top of first hdc, ch 1, hdc in same st, 2 hdc in each stitch around. (20)

Round 3: sl st to top of first hdc, ch 1, hdc in same st, hdc in next st, *2 hdc in next st, hdc in next st* repeat around. (30)

Round 4: sl st to top of first hdc, ch 1, hdc in same st, hdc in each of next 2 sts, *2 hdc in next st, hdc in each of next 2 sts* repeat around. (40)

Round 5: sl st to top of first hdc, ch 1, hdc in same st, hdc in each of next 3 sts, *2 hdc in next st, hdc in each of next 3 sts* repeat around. (50)

Round 6: sl st to top of first hdc, ch 1, hdc in same st, hdc in each of next 4 sts, *2 hdc in next st, hdc in each of next 4 sts* repeat around. (60)

Round 7: sl st to top of hdc, ch 1, hdc in same St, hdc in each of next 5 sts, *2 hdc in next st, hdc in each of next 5 sts* repeat around. (70)

Round 8: BLO (this row is to be completed in BLO) sl st to top of first hdc, ch 1, hdc in next st and around. (70)

Round 9: sl st to top of first hdc, ch 1, hdc in next st and around. (70)

Round 10: sl st to top of first hdc, ch 1, hdc in next st and around. (70)

Round 11: sl st to top of first hdc, ch 1, hdc in next st and around. (70)

Round 12: **Color B this round.** Sl st to top of first hdc, ch 1, hdc in next st and around. (70) Change back to Color A at y/o of last hdc of this round.

Round 13: BPSC around. (70)

Round 14: sl st to top of first hdc, ch 1, hdc in next st and around. (70)

Round 15: sl st to top of first hdc, ch 1, hdc in next st and around. (70)

Round 16: **Color B this round.** Sl st to top of first hdc, ch 1, hdc in next st and around. (70) Change back to Color A at y/o of last hdc of this round.

Round 17: BPSC around. (70)

Round 18: BLO, sl st to top of first hdc, ch 1, hdc in same st, hdc in each of next 6 sts, *2 hdc in next st, hdc in each of next 6 sts* repeat around. (80)

Round 19: BLO, sl st to top of first hdc, ch 1, hdc in next st and around. (80)

Round 20: BLO, sl st to top of first hdc, ch 1, hdc in same st, hdc in each of next 7 sts, *2 hdc in next st, hdc in each of next 7 sts* repeat around. (90)

Picture 3: Yarn over, pull through all loops on hook.

Picture 4: Back loop only.

Round 21: BLO, sl st to top of first hdc, ch 1, hdc in next st and around. (90)
Round 22: BLO, sl st to top of first hdc, ch 1, hdc in same st, hdc in each of next 8 sts, *2 hdc in next st, hdc in each of next 8 sts* repeat around. (100)
Round 23: BLO, sl st to top of first hdc, ch 1, hdc in next st and around. (100) Sl st to next st and F/O (turn right side out).

DAISY

Color C. Chain 3, hdc in third st from hook 10 times.
Switch to Color B.
Change colors at this point if you would like middle and petals different.
Sl st to top of ch 3, ch 4, 4 dtr, ch 3, sl st all in same space. Repeat around creating 10 petals. F/O.
Rotate petals slightly so they overlap each other on one side and continue around.
Sew to hat or attach clip to make flower removable.

Star Stitch Sundress

This cotton sundress is simply stunning! Beautiful stitching adds a nice design element while keeping the dress simple. It is fully adjustable with a ruffle at the top and a tied waist. Whether she has a party to attend or just a day outside, a girl will feel like a princess when she wears this dress.

Materials

- Cascade Ultra Pima 10 x 100g/220yds 100% Pima Cotton
  – Color #3767 / color name Deep Coral / 4 skeins
- 1 ½" ribbon for belt/sash
- **Hooks:** H (4mm)

Skill level: Advanced

Gauge: 10 sc = 2", 12 sc rows = 2"

Glossary of abbreviations

ch – chain
sc – single crochet
dc – double crochet
tr – triple or treble crochet
sl st – slip stitch
sk – skip
F/O – fasten off
(#) number of stitches at end of round
[_] to be completed in same st
* _ * to be repeated

Helpful Tips – *(sc, dc), sk 1* will be repeated numerous times during this pattern. It will form a star-like pattern on the dress. The (sc, dc) should be done in the sc of the previous row, skipping the dc of the previous row. If your pattern does not look like the picture below, this just means the (sc, dc) has been done in the (dc) wrong stitch.

SIZE AGE 2
Ch 117
Round 1: ch 2, dc in next 115 sts. (116)
Round 2–3: dc in each st around. (116)
Round 4–21: *[sc, dc], sk 1* repeat 57 more times around. (58 groups of sc, dc in total.)
Round 22: sl st to first st, ch 3, tr in each of next 115 sts. (116)
Round 23–46: *[sc, dc], sk 1* repeat 57 more times around. (58 groups of sc, dc in total.)
F/O.

SIZE AGE 3
Ch 129, sl st to first st to form circle.
Round 1: ch 2, dc in next 126 sts. (127)
Round 2–3: dc in ea st around. (127)
Round 4–26: *[sc, dc], sk 1* repeat 62 more times around. (63 groups of sc, dc in total.)
Round 27: sl st to first st, ch 3, tr in each of next 126 sts. (127)
Round 28–56: *[sc, dc], sk 1* repeat 62 more times around. (63 groups of sc, dc in total.)
F/O.

SIZE AGES 4/5

Ch 141, sl st to first st to form circle.
Round 1: ch 2, dc in next 138 sts. (139)
Round 2–3: dc in ea st around. (139)
Round 4–31: *[sc, dc], sk 1* repeat 69 more times around. (70 groups of sc, dc in total.)
Round 32: sl st to first st, ch 3, tr in each of next 138 sts. (139)

Round 33–66: *[sc, dc], sk 1* repeat 69 more times around. (70 groups of sc, dc in total.)
F/O.

STRAPS (Make 4)

Ch 100.
Weave 2 straps together across front of sundress at row 3.

Leave 15 st open on each side (for underarms). (Leave 12 open for size 3; leave 10 open for size 2.)
Weave 2 straps together across back of sundress at row 3. (Picture 1)
Weave Ribbon for belt through every 2 sts of tr row.

Picture 1: Weave straps through every other stitch.

Picture 2: Pull to gather for ruffled top.

Picture 3: Insert ribbon at waist, every two stitches.

Picture 4: Use long crochet piece in place of ribbon.

Flowers

Size H hook (4mm) for Petal flower
Size N hook (10mm) for Ruffle flower
Cascade Ultra Pima:
Small amounts (less than 10 yards)
Suggested colours:
#3767 Deep Coral
#3764 Sunshine

TEN PETAL FLOWER

Start with middle color.
Round 1: ch 3, 10 dc in third st from hook. (10) (Picture 1)
Round 2: 2 sc in each of next 10 sts. (20)
Change to petal color at last y/o of previous row.
Round 3: [sl st in next st, ch 2, dc, tr, dc, ch 2], skip next st*
repeat 9 more times, creating 10 petals in total.
F/O.

Picture 1: Weave straps through every other stitch.

Picture 2: First petal of 10.

Picture 3: Ch 31, 29 hdc across.

Picture 4: Rotate chain in swirl motion.

Picture 5: Use loose ends to sew bottom of flower to secure.

RUFFLE FLOWER

Ch 31, turn.
Row 1: hdc in second st from hook, 29 hdc across
(Picture 3).
Leave tail for sewing together.
Rotate chain in swirl motion. (Picture 4).
Use loose ends to sew bottom side of flower to secure swirl. (Picture 5).

Surfer Shorts

The perfect pair of shorts for all little boys! It has always been a challenge designing something for boys that doesn't have a babyish feel to it. Surfer shorts and a shirt with surfboard appliqués will make every boy feel like a surfer dude. The yarn provides a nice weight and feel for the summer months.

Materials

- Cascade Ultra Pima 100g/220 yds 100% Cotton
  - Color #3772 / color name Cornflower (Color A) / 2 skeins
  - Color #3764 / color name Sunshine (Color B) / 1 skeins
  - Color #3723 / color name Navy (Color C) / 1 skeins

- **Hook:** H (4mm)

Skill level: Intermediate   **Gauge:** 10 sc= 2", 12 sc rows = 2"

Glossary of abbreviations

ch – chain
sc – single crochet
dc – double crochet
tr – triple or treble crochet
sl st – slip stitch
sk – skip
sp – space
F/O – fasten off
sc2tog – single crochet 2 stitches together (decrease)
y/o – yarn over
(#) number of stitches at end of round
* _ * to be repeated
[_] to be completed in same st

Create TWO panels for each pair of shorts

SIZE AGE 2
Waist 21"
Hips 21"
Color A.
Ch 48, turn.
Row 1: dc in second st from hook, 46 dc across, ch 2, turn. (47)
Row 2: 47 dc across, ch 2, turn. (47)
Row 3: 47 dc across, ch 1, turn. (47)
Row 4–12: 47 sc across, ch 1, turn. (47)
Change to Color B at last y/o of previous row.
Row 13–18: 47 sc across, ch 1, turn. (47)
Change to Color C at last y/o of previous row.
Row 19–22: 47 sc across, ch 1, turn. (47)
Change to Color B at last y/o of previous row.
Row 23–28: 47 sc across, ch 1, turn. (47)
Change to Color A at last y/o of previous row.
Row 29–49: 47 sc across, ch 1 turn. (47)
Row 50: 47 sc across.
F/O.

SIZE AGES 3/4
Waist 21½"
Hips 22"
Color A.
Ch 55, turn.
Row 1: dc in second st from hook, 53 dc across, ch 2, turn. (54)
Row 2: 54 dc across, ch 2, turn. (54)
Row 3: 54 dc across, ch 1, turn. (54)
Row 4–18: 54 sc across, ch 1, turn. (54)
Change to Color B at last y/o of previous row.
Row 19–25: 54 sc across, ch 1, turn. (54)
Change to Color C at last y/o of previous row
Row 26–29: 54 sc across, ch 1, turn. (54)
Change to Color B at last y/o of previous row.
Row 30–36: 54 sc across, ch 1, turn. (54)
Change to Color A at last y/o of previous row.
Row 37–59: 54 sc across, ch 1 turn. (54)
Row 60: 54 sc across. (54)
F/O.

SIZE AGE 5
Waist 22"
Hips 23"
Color A
Ch 65, turn.
Row 1: dc in second st from hook, 63 dc across, ch 2, turn. (64)

Row 2–3: 64 dc across, ch 2, turn. (64)
Row 4: 64 dc across, ch 1, turn. (64)
Row 5–18: 64 sc across. (64)
Change to Color B at last y/o of previous row.
Row 19–30: 64 sc across, ch 1, turn. (64)
Change to Color C at last y/o of previous row.
Row 31–37: 54 sc across, ch 1, turn. (64)
Change to Color B at last y/o of previous row.
Row 38–49: 64 sc across, ch 1, turn. (64)
Change to Color A at last y/o of previous row.
Row 50–74: 64 sc across, ch 1 turn. (64)
Row 75: 64 sc across. (64)
F/O.

Make 2 square tie panels:
Ch 9, turn.
Row 1–9: 8 sc across, ch 1, turn.
Row 10: 8 sc across, ch 2, turn.
Row 11: sk 2 sts, 1 sc in each of next 3 sts, ch 2, sk 2, sc last st, turn.
Row 12: 3 sc in ch 2 sp, sc in each of next 3 sts, 3 sc in ch 2 Sp, ch 1, turn.
Row 13: 9 sc across.
F/O.
Place panels on shorts so small lace holes are towards center.
Sew top, bottom and outside of panels to front of shorts.
Chain 100 for tie to weave in square tie panels.

Picture 1: Fold each panel in half and match up stripes. Overlap top of shorts to appropriate waist size measurement

Picture 2: Fold down front of shorts and sew backside. Flip shorts around and sew other side. Sew leg seams closed.

Picture 3: Make two small tie panels for front.

Picture 4: Attach to shorts and use chain to lace.

Surfboard Appliqués

Size H hook (4mm)
Cascade Ultra Pima:
Small amounts (less than 10 yards)
Suggested colors:
#3767 Deep Coral
#3764 Sunshine
#3723 Navy
#3748 Buttercup
Needle to attach embellishments

SURFBOARD

Ch 9, turn.
Row 1: sc in second st from hook, sc 7 across, ch 1, turn. (8)
Row 2–4: 8 sc across, ch 1, turn. (8)
Row 5: sc in first 3 sts, 2 dc in next st, 2 dc in next st, sc in last 3 sts, ch 1, turn. (10)
Rows 6–21: 10 sc across, ch 1, turn. (10)
Row 22: sc2tog, sc in each of next 6 sts, sc2tog, ch 1, turn. (8)
Rows 23–26: 8 sc across, ch 1, turn. (8)
Row 27: sc2tog, sc in each of next 4 sts, sc2tog, ch 1, turn. (6)
Rows 28–30: 6 sc across, ch 1, turn. (6)
Row 31: sc2tog, sc in each of next 2 sts, sc2tog (4)
Rows 32–34: 4 sc across, ch 1, turn. (4)
Rows 35: sc2tog, sc2tog, ch 1, turn. (2)
Rows 36–37: 2 sc across, ch 1, turn. (2)
Row 38: sc2tog. (1)
F/O.

HALF FLOWER

Start with middle color.
Round 1: ch 3, 5 dc in third st from hook, ch 1, turn. (5) (Picture 1)
Round 2: 2 sc in each of next 5 sts. Turn. (10)
Change to petal color at last y/o of previous row.
Round 3: *[sl st in next st, ch 2, dc, tr, dc, ch 2], skip next st* repeat 4 more times, creating 5 petals total. (Picture 2)
F/O.

STRIPE

Ch 36.
Sew to surfboard appliqué.
(Picture 3)

Picture 1: 5 dc in 3rd from hook, turn.

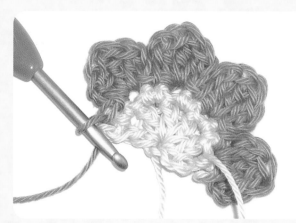

Picture 2: Complete 5 petals.

Picture 3: Close up of surfboard appliqués.

Hooded Vest with Pocket

The sleeveless cotton vest will add a little warmth and color to any outfit. Made with the selected yarn below, the silk/cotton combo feels great.

Materials

- Cascade Pima Silk 10 x 50g/109 yds 85% Peruvian Pima Cotton 15% Silk
  - Color #5141 / color name Lapis / 5 skeins (Color A)
  - Color #5134 / color name Gold / 2 skeins (Color B)
- Hook: H (5mm)

Skill level: Easy

Gauge: Size 5mm hook, 8 sc = 2", 8 sc rows = 2"

Glossary of abbreviations

sc – single crochet
dc – double crochet
sl st – slip stitch
sk – skip
FLO – front loop only
F/O – fasten off
(#) number of stitches at end of round
* _ * to be repeated (repeat)

Helpful Tips – *This vest is worked from top to bottom, creating one shoulder strap, then across the neckline, then the body of the vest.*

SIZE AGES 3/4
FRONT AND BACK
With Color A, ch 9.
Rows 1–7: sc in second st from hook and 7 across, ch 1, turn.
Row 8: sc in second st from hook, 7 across and ch 30, turn.
Row 9: sc in second st from hook, 36 sc across, ch 1, turn.
Rows 11–26: sc 37 across, ch 1, turn.
Row 27: 37 sc across, ch 5, turn.
Row 28: sc second st from hook, 44 sc across, ch 1, turn.
Rows 29–70: 45 sc across, ch 1, turn.
F/O.
Opposite shoulder strap/sleeve
Row 1: Connect to right corner and 8 sc across, ch 1, turn.
Rows 2–8: 8 sc across.
Connect front and back panels with sl st at sides and top of shoulder straps. Sc around arm openings for a smooth finish.

SIZE AGES 5/6
With Color A, ch 9.
Rows 1–8: sc in second st from hook and 7 across, ch 1, turn.
Row 9: sc in second st from hook, 7 across and ch 30, turn.
Row 10: sc in second st from hook, 36 sc across, ch 1, turn.
Rows 11–29: sc 37 across, ch 1, turn.
Row 30: 37 sc across, ch 5, turn.
Row 31: sc second st from hook, 44 sc across, ch 1, turn.
Rows 32–78: 45 sc across, ch 1, turn.
F/O.
Opposite shoulder strap/sleeve
Row 1: Connect to right corner and 8 sc across, ch 1, turn.
Rows 2–8: 8 sc across.
Connect front and back panels with sl st at sides and top of shoulder straps. Sc around arm openings for a smooth finish.

WAIST BAND
With Color A, ch 7.
Row 1–95: FLO, 7 sc across, ch 1, turn. Slip stitch together to form large circle. With 'right side' of vest facing out, line up waist band with vest bottom and slip stitch together. (Picture 1)
Fold waist band down. (Picture 2)

HOOD
Alternate colors every two rows.
Row 1: Find center of vest front, sl st, ch 2, dc across neckline (approx 74 dc), ch 2, turn. (Picture 3)
Rows 2–22: 75 dc across, ch 2, turn.
Fold top of hood in half and attach with slip stitch. (Picture 4)

POCKET
Alternate colors every two rows. Ch 31.
Rows 1–12: 30 dc across, ch 2, turn.
Stitch top and bottom of pocket to front of vest.

Picture 1: Place waist band around bottom of vest.

Picture 2: Stitch to bottom and fold over.

Picture 3: Leave front of hood open.

Picture 4: Stitch top of hood at top.

Laced-up Tankini *5-7 years*

A two-piece suit that isn't too revealing is a great addition to a little girl's summer wardrobe. Laced-up ties allow for sizing adjustments. Whether she is at the beach or playing in the backyard, she will love wearing this suit.

Materials

- Cascade Luna 10 X 50g/82 yds 100% Peruvian Cotton
  - Color #754 / color name Turquoise / 3 skein (Color A)
  - Color #728 / color name Lime / 1 skeins (Color B)
- Yarn needle
- Scissors
- **Hook:** H (5mm)

Skill level: Easy

Gauge: 7 sc= 2", 8 rows sc= 2"

Glossary of abbreviations

ch – chain
sc – single crochet
dc – double crochet
sl st – slip stitch
sk – skip
sp – space
y/o – yarn over
hdc – half double crochet
hdc dec – half double crochet decrease
F/O – fasten off
(#) number of stitches at end of round/row
Round – continues in a circle
Row – will go back and forth

SIZE: Because of the lace-up sides and back, this tankini size can range from size ages 5–7.

BIKINI BOTTOM

(Bottoms start at top of back and decrease in between legs, increasing back up frontside.)

Row 1: ch 4, hdc in fourth st from hook, ch 30, turn. (Picture 1)
Row 2: hdc in fourth st from hook, 25 hdc across, ch 3, turn. (Picture 2)
Row 3: hdc in fourth st from hook, 27 hdc across, ch 3, turn.
Row 4: hdc in fourth st from hook, 27 hdc across, ch 3, turn.
Row 5: hdc in fourth st from hook, 27 hdc across, ch 3, turn.
Row 6: hdc in fourth st from hook, 27 hdc across, ch 3, turn.
Gauge check: crochet piece measure 8½" after row 6. (Picture 3)
Row 7: hdc in fourth st from hook, 27 hdc across, ch 3, turn.

Row 8: hdc in fourth st from hook, 27 hdc across, ch 3, turn.
Row 9: hdc in second st from hook, 27 hdc across, ch 3, turn.
Row 10: hdc in second st from hook, 27 hdc across, ch 3, turn.
Row 11: hdc in second st from hook, 27 hdc across, ch 1, turn.
Row 12: hdc dec, 24 hdc across, hdc dec, ch 1, turn. (26)
Row 13: hdc dec, 22 hdc across, hdc dec, ch 1, turn. (24)
Row 14: hdc dec, 20 hdc across, hdc dec, turn. (22)
Row 15: sl st in next 5, ch 1, hdc in nx 12, leave last 5 sts unworked, ch 1, turn. (12)
Row 16: hdc dec, 8 hdc, hdc dec, turn. (10)
Row 17: hdc dec, 6 hdc, hdc dec, turn. (8)

Row 18: 8 hdc, ch 1, turn. (9)
Row 19: 8 hdc, ch 1, turn. (9)
Row 20: hdc dec, 4 hdc, hdc dec, turn. (7)
Row 21: 6 hdc, ch 1, turn. (7)
Row 22: 6 hdc, ch 1, turn. (7)
Row 23: 6 hdc, ch 1, turn.
Row 24: 6 hdc, ch 1, turn.
Row 25: 6 hdc, ch 3, turn.
Row 26: hdc in second st from hook, 7 hdc across, ch 3, turn.
Row 27: hdc in second st from hook, hdc in next 10, ch 3, turn. (Picture 4)
Row 28: hdc in second st from hook, hdc in next 12, ch 4, turn.
Row 29: hdc in second st from hook, hdc in next 16, ch 4, turn.
Row 30: hdc in first from hook, hdc in

Step 1: Starting the bikini bottom.

Step 2: Continue with the rows.

next 19, ch 3, turn.
Row 31: hdc in second st from hook, 21 hdc, ch 3, turn.
Row 32: hdc in fourth st from hook, 21 hdc, ch 3, turn.
Row 33: hdc in fourth st from hook, 21 hdc, ch 3, turn.
Row 34: hdc in fourth st from hook, 21 hdc, ch 3, turn.
Row 35: hdc in fourth st from hook, 21 hdc, ch 3, turn.
Row 36: hdc in fourth st from hook, 21 hdc, ch 3, turn.
Row 37: hdc in fourth st from hook, 21 hdc, ch 3, turn.
Row 38: hdc in fourth st from hook, 21 hdc, ch 3, turn.
Row 39: hdc in fourth st from hook, 21 hdc, ch 3, turn.
Row 40: hdc in fourth st from hook, 4 hdc, 12 sl st, ch 1, 4 hdc, ch 3, sl st in fourth st from hook.
F/O.

Step 3: Check the gauge, Crochet piece should measure 8 ½" after Row 6.

LACES FOR SIDE TIES – (Make 2)

Ch 170 and lace up sides of bikini bottoms. Laces will fit in holes made of 'hdc in fourth st from hook' spaces.

FINISH BOTTOM

Sl st below laces, ch 1, 14 hdc going along back of leg opening.
F/O and repeat for other side.
(Pictures 5 and 6)

Step 4: Forming the leg openings.

Step 5: Start to thread laces through the 'hdc 4th ch' holes.

Step 6: Continue to thread the lace down the entire side.

TOP

(Starts at bottom of top and decreases as it goes up.)

Row 1: ch 5, hdc in fourth st from hook, ch 65, turn.

Row 2: hdc in fourth from st hook, 61 hdc across, ch 3 turn.

Row 3–19: repeat Row 2.

Row 20: sl st in fourth st from hook, sl st next 17, ch 1, 27 hdc across, ch 1, turn (leave last 18 sts unworked).

Row 21: 27 hdc across, ch 2, turn.

Row 22–25: Repeat row 21.

Row 26: dc, dc, hdc, sc, 18 sl st, sc, hdc, dc, dc, ch 2, sl st to last.

Row 27: sl st to bottom corner of tankini. (Picture 7), 2 sl st, ch 2, 5 dc in same st, *sk 3 sts, 6 dc in next st* repeat across, forming 15 shells. Turn.

Row 28: sl st next 3 sts (this will bring you to middle of first shell) (Picture 8), *sk 2, 6 dc in next st* (in between shells). Repeat for 14 shells this row (Picture 9) Turn. Change colors at last y/o.

Row 29: sl st next 3 sts (this will bring you to middle of first shell), *sk 3, 6 dc in next st* (in between shells). Repeat for 13 shells this row. Turn.

Row 30: sl st next 3 sts (this will bring you to middle of first shell), *sk 3, 6 dc in next st* (in between shells). Repeat for 12 shells this row. Turn.

F/O.

STRAPS

For Right strap: sl st in between dc of row 26, ch 150. (Picture10)

For Left strap: sl st in between dc of row 26, ch 150.

F/O chains for straps. Lace in loops.

Fall

Chevron Poncho

Donning a poncho is a perfect solution to any outfit when you need just a little extra warmth in the cooler months.

Materials

- Cascade Cash Vero, worsted weight 50g/98 yds
  55% Merino Extra Fine Wool, 33% Microfiber, 12% Cashmere
  Less than a skein of each:
  – Color #21 / color name Chocolate (Color A)
  – Color #40 / color name Magenta (Color B)
  – Color #41 / color name Light Brown (Color C)
  – Color #39 / color name Bright Blue (Color D)
  – Color #26 / color name Red (Color E)
  – Color #14 / color name Purple (Color F)
  – Color #4 / color name Yellow (Color G)
  – Color #26 / color name Orange (Color H)

- **Hook:** K (6.5mm)

Skill level: Easy   **Gauge:** 7 dc =2", 3 rows dc = 2"

Glossary of abbreviations

ch – chain
sc – single crochet
dc – double crochet
sl st – slip stitch
sk – skip
F/O – fasten off
y/o – yarn over
(#) Number of stitches at end
  of round
[_] to be completed in same st
* _ * to be repeated

Helpful Tips – Change colors at last y/o of previous row.
Size age 2 – Will have 6 peaks and valleys
Size ages 3/4 – Will have 7 peaks and valleys
Size age 5 – Will have 8 peaks and valleys

SIZE AGE 2

Begin with Color A, ch 84. Connect with sl st to form circle. (Picture 1)
Round 1: dc in same st and 83 sts around.
Round 2: Color B, *4 dc in first st, 1 dc in each of next 5 sts, sk 3, 1 dc in each of next 5 sts* repeat 5 more times. (Picture 2)
Round 3: Color C, *4 dc in first st, 1 dc in each of next 5 sts, sk 3, 1 dc in each of next 5 sts* repeat 5 more times.
Round 4: Color D, *4 dc in first st, 1 dc in each of next 5 sts, sk 3, 1 dc in each of next 5 sts* repeat 5 more times.
Round 5: Color A, *4 dc in first st, 1 dc in each of next 5 sts, sk 3, 1 dc in each

of next 5 sts* repeat 5 more times.
Round 6: Color F, *4 dc in first st, 1 dc in each of next 5 sts, sk 3, 1 dc in each of next 5 sts* repeat 5 more times.
Round 7: Color C, *4 dc in first st, 1 dc in each of next 5 sts, sk 3, 1 dc in each of next 5 sts* repeat 5 more times.
Round 8: Color G, *4 dc in first st, 1 dc in each of next 5 sts, sk 3, 1 dc in each of next 5 sts* repeat 5 more times.
Round 9: Color A, *4 dc in first st, 1 dc in each of next 5 sts, sk 3, 1 dc in each of next 5 sts* repeat 5 more times.
Round 10: Color H, *4 dc in first st, 1 dc in each of next 5 sts, sk 3, 1 dc in each of next 5 sts* repeat 5 more times.
Round 11: Color C, *4 dc in first st, 1 dc

in each of next 5 sts, sk 3, 1 dc in each of next 5 sts* repeat 5 more times.
Round 12: Color B, *4 dc in first st, 1 dc in each of next 5 sts, sk 3, 1 dc in each of next 5 sts* repeat 5 more times. (Picture 2)
Round 13: Color C, *4 dc in first st, 1 dc in each of next 5 sts, sk 3, 1 dc in each of next 5 sts* repeat 5 more times. F/O.
Weave small piece of yarn to stitch points together at top to form shoulders (Picture 3), or leave open.

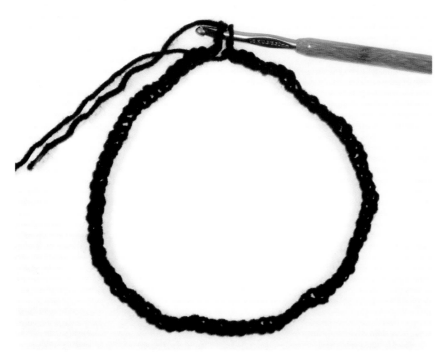

Picture 1: Slip stitch to first chain to form circle.

Picture 2: End of Round 2.

SIZE AGES 3/4

Begin with Color A, Chain 98, Connect with sl st to form circle. (Picture 1)

Round 1: dc in same st and 97 sts around.

Round 2: Color B, *4 dc in first st, 1 dc in each of next 5 sts, sk 3, 1 dc in each of next 5 sts* repeat 6 more times. (Picture 2)

Round 3: Color C, *4 dc in first st, 1 dc in each of next 5 sts, sk 3, 1 dc in each of next 5 sts* repeat 6 more times.

Round 4: Color D, *4 dc in first st, 1 dc in each of next 5 sts, sk 3, 1 dc in each of next 5 sts* repeat 6 more times.

Round 5: Color A, *4 dc in first st, 1 dc in each of next 5 sts, sk 3, 1 dc in each of next 5 sts* repeat 6 more times.

Round 6: Color F, *4 dc in first st, 1 dc in each of next 5 sts, sk 3, 1 dc in each of next 5 sts* repeat 6 more times.

Round 7: Color C, *4 dc in first st, 1 dc in each of next 5 sts, sk 3, 1 dc in each of next 5 sts* repeat 6 more times.

Round 8: Color G, *4 dc in first st, 1 dc in each of next 5 sts, sk 3, 1 dc in each of next 5 sts* repeat 6 more times.

Round 9: Color A, *4 dc in first st, 1 dc in each of next 5 sts, sk 3, 1 dc in each of next 5 sts* repeat 6 more times.

Round 10: Color H, *4 dc in first st, 1 dc in each of next 5 sts, sk 3, 1 dc in each of next 5 sts* repeat 6 more times.

Round 11: Color C, *4 dc in first st, 1 dc in each of next 5 sts, sk 3, 1 dc in each of next 5 sts* repeat 6 more times.

Round 12: Color B, *4 dc in first st, 1 dc in each of next 5 sts, sk 3, 1 dc in each of next 5 sts* repeat 6 more times. (Picture 2)

Round 13: Color C, *4 dc in first st, 1 dc in each of next 5 sts, sk 3, 1 dc in each of next 5 sts* repeat 6 more times. F/O.

Weave small piece of yarn to stitch points together at top to form shoulders (Picture 3), or leave open.

SIZE 5

Begin with Color A, Chain 112,
Connect with sl st to form circle.
(Picture 1)

Round 1: dc in same st and 111 sts
around.

Round 2: Color B, *4 dc in first st, 1 dc
in each of next 5 sts, sk 3, 1 dc in each
of next 5 sts* repeat 7 more times.
(Picture 2)

Round 3: Color C, *4 dc in first st, 1 dc
in each of next 5 sts, sk 3, 1 dc in each
of next 5 sts* repeat 7 more times.

Round 4: Color D, *4 dc in first st, 1 dc
in each of next 5 sts, sk 3, 1 dc in each
of next 5 sts* repeat 7 more times.

Round 5: Color A, *4 dc in first st, 1 dc
in each of next 5 sts, sk 3, 1 dc in each
of next 5 sts* repeat 7 more times.

Round 6: Color F, *4 dc in first st, 1 dc
in each of next 5 sts, sk 3, 1 dc in each
of next 5 sts* repeat 7 more times.

Picture 3: Stitch top together where arrows indicate to form 'shoulders'.

Round 7: Color C, *4 dc in first st, 1 dc in each of next 5 sts, sk 3, 1 dc in each of next 5 sts* repeat 7 more times.
Round 8: Color G, *4 dc in first st, 1 dc in each of next 5 sts, sk 3, 1 dc in each of next 5 sts* repeat 7 more times.
Round 9: Color A, *4 dc in first st, 1 dc in each of next 5 sts, sk 3, 1 dc in each of next 5 sts* repeat 7 more times.
Round 10: Color H, *4 dc in first st, 1 dc in each of next 5 sts, sk 3, 1 dc in each of next 5 sts* repeat 7 more times.
Round 11: Color C, *4 dc in first st, 1 dc in each of next 5 sts, sk 3, 1 dc in each of next 5 sts* repeat 7 more times.
Round 12: Color B, *4 dc in first st, 1 dc in each of next 5 sts, sk 3, 1 dc in each of next 5 sts* repeat 7 more times. (Picture 2)
Round 13: Color C, *4 dc in first st, 1 dc in each of next 5 sts, sk 3, 1 dc in each of next 5 sts* repeat 7 more times.
Round 14: Color D, *4 dc in first st, 1 dc in each of next 5 sts, sk 3, 1 dc in each of next 5 sts* repeat 7 more times.
Round 15: Color A, *4 dc in first st, 1 dc in each of next 5 sts, sk 3, 1 dc in each of next 5 sts* repeat 6 more times.
Round 16: Color F, *4 dc in first st, 1 dc in each of next 5 sts, sk 3, 1 dc in each of next 5 sts* repeat 6 more times. F/O.
Weave small piece of yarn to stitch points together at top to form shoulders (Picture 3), or leave open.

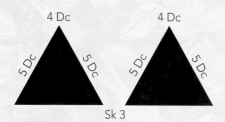

Houndstooth Fedora

The Houndstooth Fedora is a classic look for both boys and girls any time of the year. By using two strands of the cotton, it provides extra thickness to the hat and the brim can be molded to any style you desire.

Materials

- Cascade Ultra Pima 100g/220 yds #5 medium weight 100% Cotton
  - Color #3724 / color name Armada / 2 skeins (Color A)
  - Color #3728 / color name White / 1 skein (Color B)
- **Hook:** H (5mm)

Skill level: Advanced

Gauge: 2" Circle at end of round 3. (30 hdc)

Glossary of abbreviations

ch – chain
hdc – half double crochet
dc – double crochet
sl st – slip stitch
sk – skip
F/O – fasten off
y/o – yarn over
(#) number of stitches at end of round
* _ * to be repeated
Round – continues in a circle

Helpful Tips – Work the hat by holding 2 strands of yarn together. Color changes should be at last y/o over previous row.

Houndstooth design is created with a sl st in one st and a dc in the following st. This picture shows the dc being completed, a sl st will be the next st made.

HAT
Holding 2 strands of Color A together:
Round 1: ch 2, 10 hdc in second st from hook. (10)
Round 2: 2 hdc in each st around. (20)
Round 3: *2 hdc in first st, 1 hdc in next st* repeat around. (30)
Round 4: *2 hdc in first st, 1 hdc in each of next 2 sts* repeat around. (40)
Round 5: *2 hdc in first st, 1 hdc in each of next 3 sts* repeat around. (50)
Round 6: *2 hdc in first st, 1 hdc in each of next 4 sts* repeat around. (60)
Round 7: *2 hdc in first st, 1 hdc in each of next 5 sts* repeat around. (70)

Round 8: *2 hdc in first st, 1 hdc in each of next 6 sts* repeat around. (80)
Gauge check: circle measures 5½" across
Round 9: Color B, *sl st in first st, dc in next st* repeat around. (80)
Round 10: Color A, *sl st in first st, dc in next st* repeat around. (80)
Round 11: Color B, *sl st in first st, dc in next st* repeat around. (80)
Round 12: Color A, *sl st in first st, dc in next st* repeat around. (80)
Round 13: Color B, *sl st in first st, dc in next st* repeat around. (80)
Round 14: Color A, *sl st in first st, dc in next st* repeat around. (80)
Round 15: Color B, *sl st in first st, dc in next st* repeat around. (80)
Round 16: Color A, *sl st in first st, dc in next st* repeat around. (80)
Round 17: Color B, *sl st in first st, dc in next st* repeat around. (80)
Round 18: Color A, *sl st in first st, dc in next st* repeat around. (80)
Round 19: Color B, *sl st in first st, dc in next st* repeat around. (80)
Round 20: Color A, *sl st in first st, dc in next st* repeat around. (80)
Round 21: Color B, *sl st in first st, dc in next st* repeat around. (80)
Round 22: Color A, *sl st in first st, dc in next st* repeat around. (80)
Round 23: Color B, *sl st in first st, dc in next st* repeat around. (80)
Round 24: Color A, *2 hdc in first st, 1 hdc in each of next 7 sts* repeat around. (90)
Round 25: hdc around. (90)
Round 26: *2 hdc in first st, 1 hdc in each of next 8 sts* repeat around. (100)
Round 27: hdc around. (100)
Round 28: *2 hdc in first st, 1 hdc in each of next 9 sts* repeat around. (110) F/O.

Shape Hat by rolling up back and sides of brim. Push down middle to form crease.

School Cardigan

The school cardigan is a great item to have for the Fall months. Not quite cold enough to bring out your heavy coat, but there's still a brisk feel to the air. With the textured design around the chest, this sweater provides an extra layer of warmth. Striped elbow patches are a ton of fun. With so many color options, it would be great in school or team colors!

Materials

- Cascade Eco Alpaca 100g/220 yds 100% Natural Undyed Alpaca
  – Color #1512 / color name Camel / 4 skeins (Color A)
  – Color #1520 / color name Black / 1 skein (Color B)
  – Color #3003 / color name Ruby / 1 skein (Color C)
- 3 buttons
- **Hooks:** G (4mm)

Skill level: Advanced

Gauge: 9 alternating FPDC/BPDC = 2",
6 Rows alternating FPDC/BPDC = 2"

Glossary of abbreviations

Terms
ch – chain
hdc – half double crochet
sl st – slip stitch
sk – skip
hdc dec – half double crochet
  decrease (combining 2 sts to
  make 1)
F/O – fasten off
FPDC – Front Post double
  crochet (Double crochet from
  the front side of the post)
BPDC – Back Post double
  crochet (Double crochet from
  the backside of the post)
(#) number of stitches at end of
  round
* _ * to be repeated
Round – continues in a circle
Row – goes back and forth

Helpful Tips – By alternating stitches with a Front Post double crochet and a Back Post double crochet, you will give your garment a nice texture and a little more thickness. (Picture 1)

This sweater is created with six basic sections:
- Right Front Panel
- Left Front Panel
- Back Panel
- Sleeves
- Trim
- Elbow Patches

ELBOW PATCHES (PICTURE 1)
Color C
Ch 5, turn.
Row 1: dc in second st from hook, 2 dc in next st, dc in each of next 2, ch 2, turn.
Row 2: 3 dc in third st from hook, dc in each of next 3, 4 dc last, ch 2, turn.
Color B
Row 3: 2 dc in third st from hook, dc in each of next 8, 3 dc last, ch 2, turn.
Row 4: dc third st from hook, dc in each of next 11, 2 dc last, ch 2, turn.
Color C
Row 5: dc third st from hook, dc in each of next 13, 2 dc last, ch 2, turn.
Row 6: dc fourth st from hook, dc in each of next 13, dc last, ch 2, turn.
Color B
Row 7: dc third st from hook, dc dec, dc in each of next 10, dc dec, ch 2, turn.
Row 8: dc third st from hook, dc dec 2 times, dc in each of next 5, dc dec 2 times, ch 2, turn.
Color C
Row 9: dc dec, dc in each of next 6, dc dec, ch 2, turn.
Row 10: dc dec 4 times. F/O.
With color B, sc around oval .

SIZE AGES 2/3
FRONT PANELS (Make 2)
Ch 10.

Row 1: dc in second st from hook, dc in each of next 8 sts, ch 3, turn.
Row 2: *FPDC, BPDC* repeat 4 more times, ch 3, turn. (10)
Row 3: *BPDC, FPDC* repeat 4 more times, BPDC in last stitch, ch 3, turn. (11)
Row 4: *FPDC, BPDC* repeat 5 more times, ch 3, turn. (12)
Row 5: *BPDC, FPDC* repeat 5 more times, FPDC in last stitch, ch 3, turn. (13)
Row 6: *FPDC, BPDC* repeat 6 more times, ch 3, turn. (14)
Row 7: *BPDC, FPDC* repeat 6 more times, BPDC in last stitch, ch 3, turn. (15)
Row 8: *FPDC, BPDC* repeat 7 more times, ch 3, turn. (16)
Row 9: *BPDC, FPDC* repeat 7 more times, FPDC in last stitch, ch 3, turn. (17)
Row 10: *FPDC, BPDC* repeat 8 more times, ch 3, turn. (18)
Row 11: *BPDC, FPDC* repeat 8 more times, BPDC in last stitch, ch 3, turn. (19)
Row 12: *FPDC, BPDC* repeat 9 more times, ch 3, turn. (20)
Row 13: *BPDC, FPDC* repeat 9 more times, FPDC in last stitch, ch 3, turn. (21)
Row 14: *FPDC, BPDC* repeat 10 more times, ch 3, turn. (22)
Row 15: *BPDC, FPDC* repeat 10 more times, BPDC in last stitch, ch 3, turn. (23)
Row 16: *FPDC, BPDC* repeat 11 more times, ch 3, turn. (24)
Row 17: *BPDC, FPDC* repeat 11 more times, FPDC in last stitch, ch 3, turn. (25)
Row 18: skip first post, *BPDC, FPDC* repeat 11 more times, BPDC in last stitch, ch 3, turn. (25)
Row 19: skip first post, *FPDC, BPDC* repeat 11 more times, FPDC in last stitch, ch 3, turn. (25
Row 20–45: Repeat Rows 18 and 19, alternating each row. (25)
(Odd numbered rows will start with a

Picture 1: Elbow patch.

FPDC, even numbered rows will start with a BPDC.)
Row 46: skip first post, *BPDC, FPDC* repeat 11 more times, BPDC in last stitch. (25) F/O.

BACK PANEL
Ch 43.
Row 1: dc in second st from hook, dc in each of next 41 stitches, ch 3, turn. (42)
Row 2: skip first post *FPDC, BPDC* repeat 20 more times, ch 3, turn. (42)
Rows 3–45: Repeat row 2. (42)
Row 46: *FPDC, BPDC* repeat 4 more times, ch 3, turn. (10)
Rows 47–48: skip first post, *FPDC, BPDC* repeat 4 more times, ch 3, turn. (10)
Row 49: skip first post, *FPDC, BPDC* repeat 4 more times. (10) F/O.
Row 1: Slip Stitch to top right corner of main panel (opposite side, across from rows 46–49), ch 3, skip first post, *BPDC, FPDC* repeat 4 more times, ch 3, turn. (10)
Rows 2–3: skip first post, *BPDC, FPDC* repeat 4 more times, ch 3, turn. (10)
Row 4: skip first post, *BPDC, FPDC* repeat 4 more times, ch 3, turn. (10)
Attach front and back panels, leaving approx 5½" to 6" opening for armholes.

SLEEVES
Round 1: sl st to bottom of armhole, 50 hdc around. (50)
Round 2: hdc dec, 48 hdc around. (49)
Round 3: hdc dec, 47 hdc around. (48)
Rounds 4–21: hdc dec, hdc around. (This will decrease each row by one stitch.)
Rounds 22–33: 30 hdc around. (30)
Change to Color B.
Round 34: 30 hdc around. (30)
Change to Color C.
Round 35: 30 sc around. (30)
Change to Color B.
Round 36: 30 hdc around. (30)

TRIM
The number of stitches may vary slightly depending on how close you space them. Make them evenly spaced. If you place too many stitches around it may cause a ruffle effect, not enough stitches may cause sweater to pucker from the tight trim.
Color B.
Row 1: sl st to bottom/middle corner of front panel, complete 180 hdc up front panel, round collar and back down opposite panel, 80 hdc across entire bottom. (180)
Row 2: 180 hdc up one side of front, around collar, down opposite side, ch 1, turn. (180)
Row 3: 180 hdc up one side of front, around collar, down opposite side, ch 1, turn. (180)
Change to Color C.

Row 4: 180 sc up one side of front, around collar, down opposite side, ch 1, turn. (180)
Row 5: *10 sc, sk next 4 stitches, ch 4* repeat 2 more times to form button holes, sc up remaining stitches on front and collar, ch 1, turn.
Row 6: sc up one side of front, around collar, down opposite side, ch 1, turn. (180)
Change to Color B.
Rows 7–9: 180 hdc around front of sweater. (180) F/O.

SIZE AGES 4/5
FRONT PANELS (Make 2)
Ch 10.
Row 1: dc in second st from hook, dc in each of next 8 sts, ch 3, turn.
Row 2: *FPDC, BPDC* repeat 4 more times, ch 3, turn. (11)

Picture 1: Close up of back neckline.

Row 3: *BPDC, FPDC* repeat 4 more times, BPDC in last stitch, ch 3, turn. (11)
Row 4: *FPDC, BPDC* repeat 5 more times, ch 3, turn. (12)
Row 5: *BPDC, FPDC* repeat 5 more times, FPDC in last stitch, ch 3, turn. (13)
Row 6: *FPDC, BPDC* repeat 6 more times, ch 3, turn. (14)
Row 7: *BPDC, FPDC* repeat 6 more times, BPDC in last stitch, ch 3, turn. (15)
Row 8: *FPDC, BPDC* repeat 7 more times, ch 3, turn. (16)
Row 9: *BPDC, FPDC* repeat 7 more times, FPDC in last stitch, ch 3, turn. (17)
Row 10: *FPDC, BPDC* repeat 8 more times, ch 3, turn. (18)
Row 11: *BPDC, FPDC* repeat 8 more times, BPDC in last stitch, ch 3, turn. (19)
Row 12: *FPDC, BPDC* repeat 9 more times, ch 3, turn. (20)
Row 13: *BPDC, FPDC* repeat 9 more times, FPDC in last stitch, ch 3, turn. (21)
Row 14: *FPDC, BPDC* repeat 10 more times, ch 3, turn. (22)
Row 15: *BPDC, FPDC* repeat 10 more times, BPDC in last stitch, ch 3, turn. (23)
Row 16: *FPDC, BPDC* repeat 11 more times, ch 3, turn. (24)
Row 17: *BPDC, FPDC* repeat 11 more times, FPDC in last stitch, ch 3, turn. (25)
Row 18: *FPDC, BPDC* repeat 12 more times, ch 3, turn. (26)
Row 19: *BPDC, FPDC* repeat 12 more times, BPDC in last stitch, ch 3, turn. (27)
Row 20: skip first post, *BPDC, FPDC* repeat 12 more times, BPDC in last stitch, ch 3, turn. (27)
Row 21: skip first post, *FPDC, BPDC* repeat 11 more times, FPDC in last stitch, ch 3, turn. (27)
Row 22–50: Repeat Rows 18 and 19, alternating each row. (27)
(Odd numbered rows will start with a FPDC, even numbered rows will start with a BPDC.)
Row 51: skip first post, *BPDC, FPDC* repeat 11 more times, BPDC in last stitch. (27) F/O.

BACK PANEL
Ch 53.
Row 1: dc in second st from hook, dc in each of next 51 stitches, ch 3, turn. (52)
Row 2: skip first post *FPDC, BPDC* repeat 25 more times, ch 3, turn. (52)
Rows 3–50: Repeat row 2. (52)
Row 51: *FPDC, BPDC* repeat 4 more times, ch 3, turn. (10)
Rows 52–55: skip first post, *FPDC, BPDC* repeat 4 more times, ch 3, turn. (10)
Row 56: skip first post, *FPDC, BPDC* repeat 4 more times (10) F/O
Row 1: sl st to top right corner of main panel (opposite side, across from rows 46–49), ch 3, skip first post, *BPDC, FPDC* repeat 4 more times, ch 3, turn. (10)
Rows 2–5: skip first post, *BPDC, FPDC* repeat 4 more times, ch 3, turn. (10)
Row 6: skip first post, *BPDC, FPDC* repeat 4 more times, ch 3, turn. (10)
Attach front and back panels, leaving 6" opening for armholes.

Picture 3: Button holes.

Picture 4: Attach buttons to line up with holes.

SLEEVES

Round 1: sl st to bottom of armhole, 55 hdc around. (55)
Round 2: hdc dec, 53 hdc around. (54)
Round 3: hdc dec, 52 hdc around. (53)
Rounds 4–21: hdc dec, hdc around. (This will decrease each row by one stitch.)
Rounds 22–38: 30 hdc around. (35)
Change to Color B.
Round 39: 30 hdc around. (35)
Change to Color C.
Round 40: 30 sc around. (35)
Change to Color B.
Round 41: 30 hdc around. (35)

TRIM

The number of stitches may vary slightly depending on how close you space them. Make them evenly spaced. If you place too many stitches around it may cause a ruffle effect, not enough stitches may cause the sweater to pucker from the tight trim. Color B.
Row 1: sl st to bottom/middle corner of front panel, complete 180 hdc up front panel, round collar and back down opposite panel, 90 hdc across entire bottom. (190)
Row 2: 190 hdc up one side of front, around collar, down opposite side, ch 1, turn. (190)
Row 3: 190 hdc up one side of front, around collar, down opposite side, ch 1, turn. (190)
Change to Color C.
Row 4: 190 sc up one side of front, around collar, down opposite side, ch 1, turn. (190)
Row 5: *12 sc, sk next 4 stitches, ch 4* repeat 2 more times to form button holes, sc up remaining stitches on front and collar, ch 1, turn.
Row 6: sc up one side of front, around collar, down opposite side, ch 1, turn. (190)
Change to Color B.
Rows 7–9: 190 hdc around front of sweater. (190) F/O.

Ruffle Cardigan

When I first saw this yarn, I fell in love with the softness. As the sweet lady in my local yarn shop said, "It's like crocheting a kitten." Using it to make this ruffle sweater immediately came to mind. I pictured it with a sweet holiday dress or even a pair of pants on a little girl. Satin ribbon tie closure adds a great touch, but you could always use your own creativity with a simple crochet chain for ties or even buttons.

Materials

- Cascade Eco Duo Alpaca 10 x 100g/197 yds
  70% Undyed Baby Alpaca / 30% Undyed Merino Wool
  – Color #1705 / color name Vanilla / 4 skeins
- Satin Ribbon for ties
- Stitch markers to mark beginning of each row
- **Hooks:** I (5.5mm)

Skill level: Advanced   **Gauge:** End of round 2 = 2" circle (30 hdc)

Glossary of abbreviations

ch – chain
hdc – half double crochet
sl st – slip stitch
sk – skip
hdc dec – half double crochet decrease (combining 2 sts to make 1)
F/O – fasten off
(#) number of stitches at end of round
* _ * to be repeated
Round – continues in a circle

SIZE AGES 2/3

Round 1: ch 2, 10 hdc in second st from hook. (10)
Round 2: 2 hdc in each st around. (20)
Round 3: *2 hdc in first st, 1 hdc in next st* repeat around. (30)
Round 4: *2 hdc in first st, 1 hdc in each of next 2 sts* repeat around. (40)
Round 5: *2 hdc in first st, 1 hdc in each of next 3 sts* repeat around. (50)
Round 6: *2 hdc in first st, 1 hdc in each of next 4 sts* repeat around. (60)
Round 7: *2 hdc in first st, 1 hdc in each of next 5 sts* repeat around. (70)
Round 8: *2 hdc in first st, 1 hdc in each of next 6 sts* repeat around. (80)
Round 9: *2 hdc in first st, 1 hdc in each of next 7 sts* repeat around. (90)
Round 10: *2 hdc in first st, 1 hdc in each of next 8 sts* repeat around. (100)
Round 11: ch 25, sk next 10 sts, hdc in each of next 30, ch 25, sk next 10 sts, hdc in each of next 50 sts. (130)
Round 12: 25 hdc in ch 25 space, hdc in each of next 30 sts, 25 hdc in ch 25 space, hdc in each of next 50 sts. (130)
Round 13: *2 hdc in first st, 1 hdc in each of next 12 sts* repeat around. (140)
Round 14: *2 hdc in first st, 1 hdc in each of next 13 sts* repeat around. (150)
Round 15: *2 hdc in first st, 1 hdc in each of next 14 sts* repeat around. (160)
Round 16: *2 hdc in first st, 1 hdc in each of next 15 sts* repeat around. (170)
Round 17: *2 dc in first st, 1 dc in each of next 2 sts* repeat around, dc last sts. (226)
Round 18: *2 dc in first st, 1 dc in each of next 2 sts* repeat around, dc last sts. (301)
Round 19: *2 dc in first st, 1 dc in each of next 2 sts* repeat around, dc last sts. (401)

SLEEVES

Round 1: sl st to bottom of armhole, 40 hdc around. (40) (Picture 3)
Round 2: hdc around.
Round 3: *hdc dec, hdc in each of next

Picture 1: Chain to form arm openings.

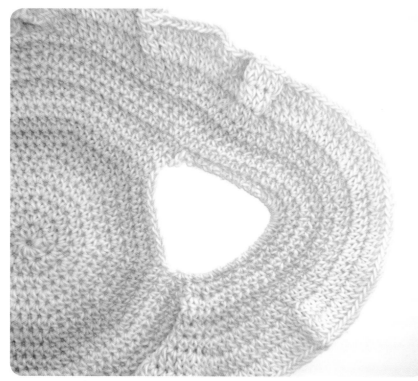

Picture 2: Half double crochet around for arm openings

3 sts* repeat (32)

Rounds 4–10: hdc around. (32)

Round 11: *hdc dec, hdc in ea of next 3 sts* repeat (24)

Rounds 12–21: 24 hdc around. (24)

Round 22: *2 dc in first st, dc in each of next 2 sts* repeat around. (32)

Round 23: *2 dc in first st, dc in each of next 2 sts* repeat around. (42)

Round 24: *2 dc in first st, dc in next st* repeat around. (56)

Round 25: 66 dc around. (56)

SIZE AGES 4/5

Round 1: ch 2, 10 hdc in second st from hook. (10)

Round 2: 2 hdc in each st around. (20)

Round 3: *2 hdc in first st, 1 hdc in next st* repeat around. (30)

Round 4: *2 hdc in first st, 1 hdc in each of next 2 sts* repeat around. (40)

Round 5: *2 hdc in first st, 1 hdc in each of next 3 sts* repeat around. (50)

Round 6: *2 hdc in first st, 1 hdc in each of next 4 sts* repeat around. (60)

Round 7: *2 hdc in first st, 1 hdc in each of next 5 sts* repeat around. (70)

Round 8: *2 hdc in first st, 1 hdc in each of next 6 sts* repeat around. (80)

Round 9: *2 hdc in first st, 1 hdc in each of next 7 sts* repeat around. (90)

Round 10: *2 hdc in first st, 1 hdc in each of next 8 sts* repeat around. (100)

Round 11: *2 hdc in first st, 1 hdc in each of next 9 sts* repeat around. (110)

Round 12: *2 hdc in first st, 1 hdc in each of next 10 sts* repeat around. (120)

Round 13: *2 hdc in first st, 1 hdc in each of next 11 sts* repeat around. (130)

Round 14: *2 hdc in first st, 1 hdc in each of next 12 sts* repeat around. (140)

Round 15: *2 hdc in first st, 1 hdc in each of next 13 sts* repeat around. (150)

Round 16: ch 35, sk 15 hdc, hdc in

each of next 80 sts, ch 35, sk 15 hdc, hdc in each of next 40 sts. (190) (Picture 1)

Round 17: hdc 35 in ch 35 space, hdc next 80 sts, hdc in ch 35 space, hdc next 40 sts. (190)

Round 18: *2 hdc in first st, hdc in each of next 18 sts* repeat around. (200)

Round 19: *2 hdc in first st, hdc in each of next 19 sts* repeat around. (210)

Round 20: *2 hdc in first st, hdc in each of next 20 sts* repeat around. (220)

Round 21: *2 hdc in first st, hdc in each of next 21 sts* repeat around. (230)

Round 22: *2 hdc in first st, hdc in each of next 22 sts* repeat around. (240)

Round 23: *2 hdc in first st, hdc in each of next 23 sts* repeat around. (250)

Round 24: *2 hdc in first st, hdc in each of next 24 sts* repeat around. (260)

Round 25: *2 hdc in first st, hdc in each of next 25 sts* repeat around. (270)

Round 26: *2 dc in first st, dc in each of next 2 sts* repeat around. (360)

Round 27: *2 dc in first st, dc in each of next 2 sts* 2 dc next st, dc last (479)

Round 28: *2 dc in first st, dc in each of next 2 sts*. (640) F/O. (Picture 2)

SLEEVES

Round 1: sl st to bottom of armhole, 50 hdc around. (50) (Picture 3)

Round 2: *hdc dec, hdc in each of next 5 sts* repeat around, hdc last 2 sts. (45)

Round 3: *hdc dec, hdc in each of next 4 sts* repeat around, hdc dec, hdc last st. (37)

Round 4: hdc dec, 35 hdc around. (36)

Rounds 5–17: 36 hdc around. (36)

Round 18: *hdc dec, hdc in each of next 4 sts* repeat around. (30)

Rounds 19–21:30 hdc around. (30)

Round 22: *hdc dec, hdc in each of next 4 sts* repeat around. (25)

Rounds 23–28: 25 hdc around.

Round 29: *2 dc in first st, dc in each of next 2 sts* repeat around. (33)

Round 30: *2 dc in first st, dc in each of next 2 sts* repeat around. (44)

Round 31: *2 dc in first st, dc in next

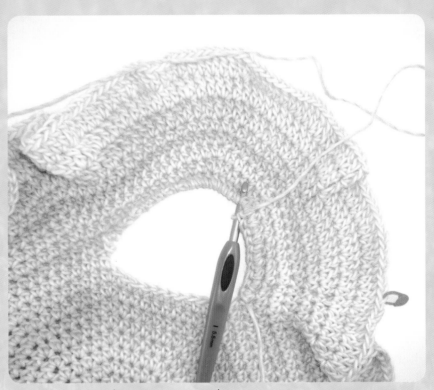

Picture 3: Sc around openings to start sleeves.

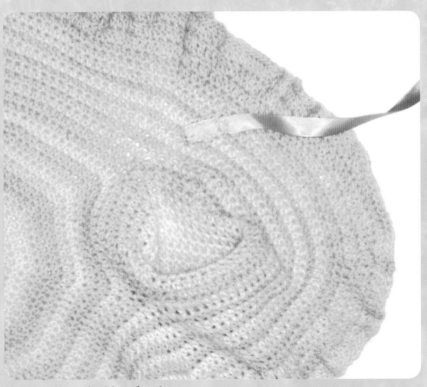

Picture 4: Attach ribbon for closure.

st* repeat around. (66)
Round 32: 66 dc around. (66)
Round 33: 66 dc around. (66) F/O.

ATTACH TIES
Sew ribbon on inside of each side of
sweater. Tie bow for closure.
(Picture 4)

Skater Sweater

This sweater was created with my 4-year-old son in mind. He is fascinated with skateboards and all things "big boys" get to do! I have come to realize that as much as I want him to stay young, I need to let him grow up. The simple design is great for all ages, with a handmade feel for someone special, yet has that "big boy coolness" factor.

Materials

- Cascade Eco Alpaca 100g/220 yds 100% Natural Undyed Alpaca
  – Color #1527 / color name Pepper Twist / 3 skeins (Color A)
  – Color #1512 / color name Camel / 1 skein (Color B)
  – Color #1520 / color name Black / 1 skein (Color C)
- **Hooks:** G (4mm) for sweater and I (5.5 mm) for ribbed edgings

Skill level: Easy   **Gauge:** 8 hdc = 2", 6 rows hdc = 2"

Glossary of abbreviations

ch – chain
hdc – half double crochet
sl st – slip stitch
sk – skip
hdc dec – half double crochet decrease (combining 2 sts to make 1)
F/O – fasten off
FLO – Front Loop Only (creates ridged effect)
y/o – yarn over
(#) number of stitches at end of round
* _ * to be repeated
Round – continues in a circle
Row – goes back and forth

***Helpful Tips** – This sweater is worked in six pieces and easily stitched together:*
- *Front Panel*
- *Back Panel*
- *Right Sleeve Cuff*
- *Left Sleeve Cuff*
- *Bottom Cuff*
- *Collar*

SIZE AGES 2/3
FRONT AND BACK PANELS
Ch 10, turn.
Row 1: hdc in second st from hook and 8 across, ch 1, turn. (10)
Row 2: 9 hdc across, ch 1, turn. (10)
Row 3: 2 hdc in second st from hook, hdc in each of next 9 sts, 2 hdc in last st. (12)
Row 4–5: 11 hdc across, ch 1, turn. (12)
Row 6: 2 hdc in second st from hook, hdc in each of next 9 sts, 2 hdc in last st, ch 33 (46)
Row 7: hdc in second st from hook, hdc in each of next 44 sts, ch 1, turn. (45)

Row 8–49: 44 hdc across, ch 1, turn. (45)
Row 50: 44 hdc across. F/O.

Row 5 – Right: Connect with sl st to top of last stitch of row 6 (Picture 1), ch 1, 10 hdc across, ch 1, turn. (12)
Row 4 – Right: 11 hdc across, ch 1, turn. (12)
Row 3 – Right: 11 hdc across, ch 1, turn. (12)
Row 2 – Right: hdc dec, hdc in each of next 7 sts, hdc dec, ch 1, turn. (10)
Row 1 – Right: 9 hdc across. F/O.

Sew Front and back panels together, leaving 5" open from top of shoulder for arm opening.

SLEEVES (Complete for each side)
Color B.
Round 1: sl st to join at bottom of armhole. Evenly space 40 sc around opening. (40)
Round 2: hdc dec, 38 hdc around. (39)
Round 3: hdc dec, 37 hdc around. (38)
Round 4: hdc dec, 36 hdc around. (37)
Round 5: hdc dec, 35 hdc around. (36)
Round 6: hdc dec, 34 hdc around. (35)

Round 7: hdc dec, 33 hdc around. (34)
Change to Color C at last y/o.
Color C.
Round 8–14: 34 hdc around. (34)
Change to Color B at last y/o.
Color B.
Round 15: hdc dec, 32 hdc around. (33)
Round 16: hdc dec, 31 hdc around. (32)
Round 17: hdc dec, 30 hdc around. (31)
Round 18: hdc dec, 29 hdc around. (30)
Round 19: hdc dec, 28 hdc around. (29)
Round 20: hdc dec, 27 hdc around. (28)
Round 21: hdc dec, 26 hdc around.
(27) F/O.

RIGHT AND LEFT SLEEVE CUFF
Color C.
Use 2 strands held together while crocheting and 5.5mm hook.
Cuffs will be worked in FLO to create ridged effect.
Ch 8, turn.
Row 1: hdc in second st from hook and 6 across, ch 1, turn. (7)
Row 2–11: FLO, 7 hdc across, ch 1, turn. (7)
Row 12: FLO, 7 hdc across, F/O.

Fold cuff in half and stitch together. (Picture 2)
Attach cuffs to right and left sleeves.

BOTTOM CUFF
Color C.
Use 2 strands held together while crocheting and 5.5mm hook.
Cuff will be worked in FLO to create ridged effect.
Ch 8, turn.
Row 1: hdc in second st from hook and 6 across, ch 1, turn. (7)
Row 2–44: FLO, 7 hdc across, ch 1, turn. (7)
Row 45: FLO, 10 hdc across, F/O.
Fold cuff in half and stitch together, attach to bottom seam. (Picture 3)

COLLAR
Color C.
Use 2 strands held together while crocheting and 5.5mm hook.
Ch 4.
Row 1: hdc in second st from hook and 2 across, ch 1, turn. (3)
Row 2–25: FLO, 4 hdc across, ch 1, turn. (3)
Row 25: FLO, 4 hdc across, F/O
Attach to sweater collar.

SIZE AGES 3/4
FRONT AND BACK PANELS
Ch 15, turn.
Row 1: hdc in second st from hook and 13 across, ch 1, turn. (15)
Row 2–4: 14 hdc across, ch 1, turn. (15)
Row 5: 2 hdc in second st from hook, hdc in each of next 14, 2 hdc in last st. (17)
Row 6–7: 16 hdc across, ch 1, turn. (17)
Row 8: 2 hdc in second st from hook, hdc in each of next 14, 2 hdc in last st, ch 40. (58)
Row 9: hdc in second st from hook, hdc in each of next 56, ch 1, turn. (57)
Row 10–55: 57 hdc across, ch 1, turn. (58)
Row 56: 57 hdc across. F/O.

Row 7 – Right: Connect with sl st to top of last stitch of Row 8 (Picture 1), ch 1, 15 hdc across, ch 1, turn. (17)
Row 6 – Right: 16 hdc across, ch 1, turn. (17)
Row 5 – Right: 16 hdc across, ch 1, turn. (17)
Row 4 – Right: hdc dec, hdc in each of next 12 sts, hdc dec, ch 1, turn. (15)
Row 3 – Right: 14 hdc across, ch 1, turn. (15)
Row 2 – Right: 14 hdc across, ch 1, turn. (15)
Row 1 – Right: 14 hdc across. F/O.

Sew Front and back panels together, leaving 6" open from top of shoulder for arm opening.

SLEEVES (Complete for each side)
Color B.
Round 1: sl st to join at bottom of armhole. Evenly space 50 sc around opening. (50)
Round 2–7: 50 hdc around. (50)
Round 8: *hdc dec, hdc in each of next 8 sts* repeat 4 more times around. (45)
Round 9: *hdc dec, hdc in each of next 8 sts* repeat 3 more times, hdc dec, hdc last 4 sts. (41)
Round 10: 41 hdc around. (41) (Change to Color C at last y/o)
Color C.
Round 11–20: 41 hdc around. (41) (Change to Color B at last y/o)
Color B.
Round 21–23: 41 hdc around. (41)
Round 24: *hdc dec, hdc in each of next 6 sts* repeat 4 more times, hdc last st (36)
Round 25–27: 36 hdc around. (36)
Round 28: *hdc dec, hdc in each of next 4 sts* repeat 5 more times. (30)
Round 29–30: 30 hdc around. F/O

RIGHT AND LEFT SLEEVE CUFF
Color C.
Use 2 strands held together while crocheting and 5.5mm hook.
Cuffs will be worked in FLO to create ridged effect.
Ch 11, turn.
Row 1: hdc in second st from hook and 9 sts across, ch 1, turn. (10)
Row 2–15: FLO, 10 hdc across, ch 1, turn. (10)
Row 16: FLO, 10 hdc across, F/O.
Fold cuff in half and stitch together. (Picture 2)
Attach cuffs to right and left sleeves.

BOTTOM CUFF
Color C.
Use 2 strands held together while crocheting and 5.5mm hook.
Cuff will be worked in FLO to create ridged effect.
Ch 11, turn.
Row 1: hdc in second st from hook and 9 sts across, ch 1, turn. (10)
Row 2–59: FLO, 10 hdc across, ch 1, turn. (10)

Picture 1: Front and back panels, attach yarn on opposite side of top to finish front.

Picture 2: Fold arm and waist band in half and stitch together before attaching.

Picture 3: Attach waistband to bottom of sweater.

Picture 4: Attach collar to top of sweater.

Row 60: FLO, 10 hdc across, F/O.
Fold cuff in half and stitch together, attach to bottom seam. (Picture 3)

COLLAR
Color C.
Use 2 strands held together while crocheting and 5.5mm hook.
Ch 5.
Row 1: hdc in second st from hook and 3 sts across, ch 1, turn. (10)
Row 2–38: FLO, 4 hdc across, ch 1, turn. (10)
Row 39: FLO, 4 hdc across, F/O.
Attach to sweater collar.

SIZE AGES 5/6
FRONT AND BACK PANELS
Ch 20, turn.
Row 1: hdc in second st from hook and 18 across, ch 1, turn. (15)
Row 2–6: 19 hdc across, ch 1, turn. (15)
Row 7: 2 hdc in second st from hook, hdc in each of next 19 sts, 2 hdc in last (22)
Row 8–9: 21 hdc across, ch 1, turn. (22)
Row 10: 2 hdc in second st from hook, hdc in each of next 19 sts, 2 hdc in last, ch 50. (73)
Row 11: hdc in second st from hook, hdc in each of next 71 sts, ch 1, turn. (72)
Row 12–60: 71 hdc across, ch 1, turn. (72)
Row 61: 57 hdc across. F/O.

Row 9 – Right: Connect with sl st to top of last stitch of Row 10 (Picture 1), ch 1, 21 hdc across, ch 1, turn. (22)
Row 8 – Right: 21 hdc across, ch 1, turn. (22)
Row 7 – Right: 21 hdc across, ch 1, turn. (22)
Row 6 – Right: 21 hdc across, ch 1, turn. (22)
Row 5 – Right: 21 hdc across, ch 1, turn. (22)
Row 4 – Right: hdc dec, hdc in each of next 17 sts, hdc dec, ch 1, turn. (20)
Row 3 – Right: 19 hdc across, ch 1, turn. (20)
Row 2 – Right: 19 hdc across, ch 1, turn. (20)
Row 1 – Right: 19 hdc across. F/O

Sew front and back panels together, leaving 6" open from top of shoulder for arm opening.

SLEEVES (Complete for each side)
Color B.
Round 1: sl st to joing at bottom of armhole. Evenly space 50 sc around opening. (50)
Round 2–9: 50 hdc around. (50)
Round 10: *hdc dec, hdc in each of next 8 sts* repeat 4 more times around. (45)
Round 11: *hdc dec, hdc in each of next 8 sts* repeat 3 more times, hdc dec, hdc last 4 sts. (41)
Round 12: 41 hdc around. (41) Change to Color C at last y/o.
Color C.
Round 13–24: 41 hdc around. (41) Change to Color B at last y/o.
Color B.
Round 25–28: 41 hdc around. (41)
Round 29: *hdc dec, hdc in each of next 6 sts* repeat 4 more times, hdc last st. (36)
Round 30–32: 36 hdc around. (36)
Round 33: *hdc dec, hdc in each of next 4 sts* repeat 5 more times. (30)
Round 34–36: 30 hdc around. F/O.

RIGHT AND LEFT SLEEVE CUFF
Color C.
Use 2 strands held together while crocheting and 5.5mm hook.
Cuffs will be worked in FLO to create ridged effect.
Ch 11, turn.
Row 1: hdc in second st from hook and 9 sts across, ch 1, turn. (10)
Row 2–16: FLO, 10 hdc across, ch 1, turn. (10)
Row 17: FLO, 10 hdc across, F/O.
Fold cuff in half and stitch together. (Picture 2)

Attach cuffs to right and left sleeves.

BOTTOM CUFF
Color C.
Use 2 strands held together while crocheting and 5.5mm hook.
Cuff will be worked in FLO to create ridged effect.
Ch 11, turn.
Row 1: hdc in second st from hook and 9 sts across, ch 1, turn. (10)
Row 2–64: FLO, 10 hdc across, ch 1, turn. (10)
Row 65: FLO, 10 hdc across, F/O.
Fold cuff in half and stitch together, attach to bottom seam. (Picture 3)

COLLAR
Color C.
Use 2 strands held together while crocheting and 5.5mm hook.
Ch 5.
Row 1: hdc in second st from hook and 3 sts across, ch 1, turn. (10)
Row 2–44: FLO, 4 hdc across, ch 1, turn. (10)
Row 45: FLO, 4 hdc across, F/O.
Fold in half and stitch together.
Attach to top of sweater.

Winter

Granny Square Winter Coat

This winter coat is created by using a classic form of crochet, the Granny Square. Two simple designs of squares are stitched together to form the shape of the coat. This is an easy project to create since you can work on each square when you have just a few spare moments. Whether you choose to do a full sleeve length or 3/4 sleeve length, the classic coat will be stylish for any girl.

Materials

- Cascade Pure Alpaca, 100g/220 yds 100% Baby Alpaca
  – Color #3003 / color name Ruby / 6 skeins (Color A)
  – Color #3036 / color name Magenta / 2 skeins (Color B)
- 2 – 1" buttons
- **Hooks:** G (4mm) for size 4 coat and H (5mm) for size 6 coat

Skill level: Intermediate

Gauge: Size 4mm hook = 2 ½" square, Size 5mm hook = 3" square

Glossary of abbreviations

ch – chain
sc – single crochet
dc – double crochet
sl st – slip stitch
sk – skip
sp – space
F/O – fasten off
y/o – yarn over
[_] to be completed in same
    st
* _ * to be repeated

Helpful Tips
Size age 4:
3 – Triangles
29 – Square 1
30 – Square 2

Size age 6:
3 – Triangles
38 – Square 1
38 – Square 2

SIZE AGE 4 AND SIZE AGE 6
SQUARE 1

With Color A, ch 2.
Round 1: 12 dc in second st from hook.
Round 2: [sl st to top of first dc, ch 2, 2 dc], ch 1, *3 dc next st, ch 1* repeat 10 more times.
Round 3: sl st to top of ch 2, sl st next st, *sl st in ch 1 sp, ch 3, sk 3 dc* repeat 11 more times.

Round 4: [sl st to ch 3 sp, ch 2, 2 sc, ch 1, 3 sc] all in ch 3 sp, 3 sc in each of next 2 ch 3 spaces, *[3 sc, ch 1, 3 sc] in next ch 3 space, 3 sc in each of next 2 ch 3 spaces* repeat 2 more times. Change to Color B at last y/o of Round 4.
Round 5: sc in each of next 3 sts, ch 1 (at corner), *sc in each of next 13 sts, ch 1* repeat one more times, sc in

each of next 10 sts, F/O.

SQUARE 2

With Color A, ch 2.
Round 1: 8 sc in second st from hook.
Round 2: sl st to top of first sc, ch 2, dc in same, ch 1 *2 dc next st, ch 1* repeat 6 more times.
Round 3: sl st to top of ch 2, [sl st to ch 1 sp, ch 2, dc, ch 1, 2 dc] all in ch 1 sp,

Square 1

Square 2

Triangle

sk next 2 dc, 2 dc in next ch 1 sp, *sk 2 dc [2 dc, ch 1, 2 dc] all in ch 1 sp, 2 dc in next ch 1 sp* repeat 2 more times.
Round 4: sl st to top of ch 2, [sl st to ch 1 sp, ch 2, dc, ch 1, 2 dc] all in ch 1 sp, sk next 2 dc, 2 dc in next ch 1 sp, 2 dc next ch 1 sp, *sk 2 dc [2 dc, ch 1, 2 dc] all in ch 1 sp, 2 dc in next ch 1 sp, 2 dc in next ch 1 sp* repeat 2 more times. Change to Color B at last y/o of Round 4.
Round 5: sc in next sp, [sc, ch 1, sc] all in ch 1 space of corner, *sc in each of

next 8 sts, [sc, ch 1, sc] in ch 1 space of corner* repeat 2 more times, sc last 7 sts. F/O.

TRIANGLE
With Color A, ch 14.
Row 1: 2 dc in second st from hook, *Ch 1, sk 2, 3 dc next st, * repeat 3 more times, turn. (5 clusters)
Row 2: sl st in second st from hook, sl st ch 1 space, ch 2, 2 dc, * ch 1, 3 dc* repeat 2 more times. (4 clusters)
Row 3: sl st in second st from hook, sl

st ch 1 space, ch 2, 2 dc, * ch 1, 3 dc* repeat 1 more time. (3 clusters)
Row 4: sl st in second st from hook, sl st ch 1 space, ch 2, 2 dc, ch 1, 3 dc. (2 clusters)
Row 5: sl st in second st from hook, sl st ch 1 space, ch 2. (1 cluster)
Change to Color B at last y/o of Row 5.
Working around triangle: ch 2, sl st to top of end cluster of Row 4, ch 2, sl st to top of end cluster of Row 3, ch 2, sl st to top of end cluster of Row 2, ch 2, sl st to top of end cluster of Row

Picture 1: Rotate start of rosette so first petal matches up to 7th petal.

Picture 2: Keep rotating, bringing each petal to center of flower.

1, 1 sc down side of Row 1 cluster, 2 sc in bottom corner of triangle. 10 sc across bottom of triangle. 2 sc corner, 1 sc side of cluster, sl st to top of end cluster of Row 1, ch 2, sl st to top of end cluster of Row 2, 1 sc down side of Row 3 cluster, ch 2, sl st to top of end cluster of Row 4, ch 2, sl st to top of end cluster of Row 5, sc on top of cluster.
F/O.

ROSETTE
With Color A, ch 51.
Row 1: 2 dc in second st from hook, *sl st in each of next 3 st, 3 dc next st* repeat for 13 petals. F/O. Leave long tail to sew flower together.
To assemble:
Turn first 7 petals to make circle. (Picture 1)
Work remaining petals into fill center opening, slightly overlapping as you go. (Picture 2)
Use long tail to stitch together to hold shape on bottom of flower.

ASSEMBLING COAT
Right Front Side
(Picture: Right Front Side)
Row 1: 1 Square in middle.
Row 2–6: 3 Squares across.
Row 7: (for size 6 coat) 3 squares across.

Left Front Side
(Picture: Left Front Side)
Row 1: 1 Square in middle.
Row 2–6: 3 Squares across.
Row 7: (for size 6 coat) 3 squares across.

	1	
1	2	1
2	1	2
1	2	1
2	1	2
1	2	1
2	1	2

Right Front side

	2	
2	1	2
1	2	1
2	1	2
1	2	1
2	1	2
1	2	1

Left Front side

BACK OF COAT

Row 1: 2 Squares across.
Row 2: 2 Squares across.
Row 3: Square, triangle, square.
Row 4–6: 4 Squares across.
Row 7: (For size 6 coat) 4 Squares across.
(Picture: Coat Back)

SLEEVE

Row 1–3: 3 Squares across.
Row 4: Triangle, 3 Squares across.
(Pictures: Sleeve Open and Sewn)

Coat Back

Sleeve open

Sleeve sewn

Winter Dress

5-6 years

The winter dress is a fun wrap style for any girl! Paired with tights and a cute colored shirt underneath, the dress can offer a formal or fun and funky style.

Materials

- Cascade Pure Alpaca, 100g/220 yds 100% Baby Alpaca
  – Color #9753 / color name Rose Mix / 5 skeins
- **Hooks:** H (5mm)

Skill level: Advanced   **Gauge:** 9 dc = 2", 4 rows of dc= 2"

Glossary of abbreviations

ch – chain
sc – single crochet
dc – double crochet
sl st – slip stitch
sk – skip
hdc – half double crochet
F/O – fasten off
(#) number of stitches at end
   of round
* _ * to be repeated (repeat)

Helpful Tips – The dress is worked in these steps:
- *Back panel*
- *Right and Left front panels*
- *Skirt*
- *Sleeves*

BRICK STITCH

Row 1: 3 dc in fourth st from hook, *sk 3 chs, sc in next st, ch 3, 3 dc in same ch.* (Picture 2 shows first ch 3 and 3 dc) Repeat across row, ending in sc.
Row 2: Chain 3 to turn, 3 dc in sc from previous row. (Picture 3)
Cont. Row 2 – *sc in next chain 3 space of previous row, ch 3, 3 dc in same chain 3 space.* (Picture 4) repeat across from *. End with single crochet in last chain 3 of previous row.

SIZE AGES 5/6
BACK

Ch 49.
Row 1: 3 dc in fourth st from hook, *sk 3 chs, sc in next st, chain 3, 3 dc in same ch.* (Picture 2 shows first ch 3 and 3 dc) Repeat across row, ending in sc. (12 'bricks')
Rows 2–21: Ch 3 to turn, 3 dc in sc from previous row. (Picture 3) (12 'bricks')

Picture 1: Close up of Brick stitch.

Picture 2: First set of 3 dc and ch 3.

Picture 3: 3 dc in sc from previous row.

Picture 4: 3 dc in ch 3 space.

Cont. Row 2 – *sc in next chain 3 space of previous row, ch 3, 3 dc in same chain 3 space.* (Picture 4) repeat across from *. End with single crochet in last chain 3 of previous row.

FRONT (Make 2)

Row 1: 3 dc in fourth chain from hook, *sk 3 chs, sc in next st, ch 3, 3 dc in same ch.* (Picture 2 shows first ch 3 and 3 dc) Repeat across row, ending in sc. (12 'bricks')
Rows 2–3: Ch 3 to turn, 3 dc in sc from previous row. (11 'bricks')
Rows 4–5: Ch 3 to turn, 3 dc in sc from previous row. (10 'bricks')
Rows 6–7: Ch 3 to turn, 3 dc in sc from previous row. (9 'bricks')
Rows 8–9: Ch 3 to turn, 3 dc in sc from previous row. (8 'bricks')
Rows 10–11: Ch 3 to turn, 3 dc in sc from previous row. (7 'bricks')
Rows 12–13: Ch 3 to turn, 3 dc in sc from previous row. (6 'bricks')
Rows 14–15: Ch 3 to turn, 3 dc in sc from previous row. (5 'bricks')
Rows 16–17: Ch 3 to turn, 3 dc in sc from previous row. (4 'bricks')
Rows18–19: Ch 3 to turn, 3 dc in sc from previous row. (3 'bricks')
Rows 20–21: Ch 3 to turn, 3 dc in sc from previous row. (2 'bricks')
Attach front panels to back at shoulder and side seams. Leave 6" opening for arms.

SKIRT

Row 1: Starting at bottom corner of one front panel, 136 sc across to other side, ch 1, turn.
Row 2: hdc second st from hook, hdc in each of next 3 sts, *2 hdc in next st, hdc in each of next 3* repeat across (166), ch 1, turn.
Row 3: 166 hdc across, ch 3, turn.
Row 4: 3 dc in fourth st from hook, *sk 3 chs, sc in next st, ch 3, 3 dc in same chain.* Repeat across row, ending in sc. (41 'bricks')
Rows 5–35: Ch 3 to turn, 3 dc in sc from

previous row, *sc in next chain 3 space of previous row, ch 3, 3 dc in same chain 3 space.* (Picture 4) repeat across from *. End with single crochet in last chain 3 of previous row.
F/O.

SLEEVES

The sleeves are worked as rows to keep with same pattern.

Row 1: 32 sc around arm opening.

Row 2: 3 dc in fourth st from hook, *sk 3 chains, sc in next chain, chain 3, 3 dc in same chain.* Repeat across row, ending in sc. (8 'bricks)

Rows 3–22: Ch 3 to turn, 3 dc in sc from previous row. (Picture 3)

Cont. Row 2 – *sc in next chain 3 space of previous row, ch 3, 3 dc in same chain 3 space.* repeat across from *. End with single crochet in last chain 3 of previous row. F/O.

Pirate Jacket

I don't know of any child that isn't fascinated by the allure of a pirate, a treasure hunt, and ships. Two strands of Pure Alpaca held together are the perfect 'worsted' thickness in yarn and will provide extra warmth. A simple wave design has been used to decorate a unique and fun jacket.

Materials

- Cascade Pure Alpaca, 100g/220 yds 100% Baby Alpaca
  - Color #3026 / color name Navy / 5 skeins (Color A)
  - Color #3023 / color name Sapphire Heather / 1 skein (Color B)
  - Color #3031 / color name Sphere / 1 skein (Color C)
- Small amounts: (For pirate ship, flag embellishments)
  - Cascade Pure Alpaca #3033 White, #3001 Black
  - Cascade Eco Duo #1704 Chicory
- 14" zipper (coil separating)
- **Hook:** J (6mm) for jacket and H (5mm) for embellishments

Skill level: Intermediate   **Gauge:** 8 sc = 2", 6 rows sc = 2"

Glossary of abbreviations

ch – chain
sc – single crochet
dc – double crochet
tr – treble (triple) crochet
sl st – slip stitch
sk – skip
FLO – Front Loop Only
sc2tog – single crochet 2 together (decrease)
F/O – fasten off
(#) number of stitches at end of round
* _ * to be repeated
Row – goes back and forth

SIZE AGES 4/5
BACK
Color A, ch 50.
Rows 1–4: sc second st from hook and 48 across, ch 1, turn.
Row 5: sc second st from hook and next 3, dc next 2, tr, dc next 2, *5 sc, 2 dc, tr, 2 dc* repeat 3 more times, ch 1, turn. (Picture 1)
Row 6: Color B, sc second st from hook, dc, 2 sc, 5 sl st, *2 sc, dc, 2 sc, 5 sl st* repeat 3 more times, ch 1, turn. (Picture 2)
Row 7: Color C, FLO sc second st from hook and 47 across, ch 1, turn. (Picture 3)
Rows 8–12: Color A, sc second st from hook and 48 across, ch 1, turn. (Picture 4)
Row 13: sc second st from hook and next 3, dc next 2, tr, dc next 2, *5 sc, 2 dc, tr, 2 dc* repeat 3 more times, ch 1, turn.
Row 14: Color B, sc second st from hook, dc, 2 sc, 5 sl st, *2 sc, dc, 2 sc, 5 sl st* repeat 3 more times, ch 1, turn.
Row 15: Color C, FLO sc second st from hook and 47 across, ch 1, turn.
Rows 16–20: sc second st from hook and 48 across, ch 1, turn.
Row 21: sc second st from hook and next 3, dc next 2, tr, dc next 2, *5 sc, 2 dc, tr, 2 dc* repeat 3 more times, ch 1, turn.
Row 22: Color B, sc second st from hook, dc, 2 sc, 5 sl st, * 2 sc, dc, 2 sc, 5 sl st* repeat 3 more times, ch 1, turn.
Row 23: Color C, FLO sc second st from hook and 47 across, ch 1, turn.
Rows 24–47: 49 sc across, ch 1, turn.

Row 48: 49 sc across (**do not** ch 1), turn.
Row 49: 9 sl st, ch 1, 32 sc, ch 1 (leave last 9 sts unworked).
Rows 50–58: 32 sc, ch 1, turn.
Rows 59–64: 8 sc, ch 1, turn.
Opposite side: repeat rows 59–64.

FRONT PANEL (Make 2)
Color A, ch 25.
Rows 1–4: sc second st from hook and 23 across, ch 1, turn.
Row 5: sc second st from hook and next 3, dc next 2, tr, dc next 2, *5 sc, 2 dc, tr, 2 dc* repeat 1 more time, ch 1, turn.
Row 6: Color B, sc second st from hook, dc, 2 sc, 5 sl st, *2 sc, dc, 2 sc, 5 sl st* repeat 1 more time, ch 1, turn.
Row 7: Color C, FLO sc second st from

*Picture 1: *5 sc, 2 dc, tr, 2 dc* repeat across.*

*Picture 2: *2 sc, dc, 2 sc, 5 sl st* repeat across.*

Picture 3: sc across, front loop only

hook and 23 across, ch 1, turn.

Rows 8–12: sc second st from hook and 23 across, ch 1, turn.

Row 13: sc second st from hook and next 3, dc next 2, tr, dc next 2, *5 sc, 2 dc, tr, 2 dc* repeat 1 more time, ch 1, turn.

Row 14: Color B, sc second st from hook, dc, 2 sc, 5 sl st, *2 sc, dc, 2 sc, 5 sl st* repeat 1 more time, ch 1, turn.

Row 15: Color C, FLO sc second st from hook and 23 across, ch 1,

Rows 16–20: sc second st from hook and 23 across, ch 1, turn.

Row 21: sc second st from hook and next 3, dc next 2, tr, dc next 2, *5 sc, 2 dc, tr, 2 dc* repeat 1 more time, ch 1, turn.

Row 22: Color B, sc second st from hook, dc, 2 sc, 5 sl st, *2 sc, dc, 2 sc, 5 sl st* repeat 1 more time, ch 1, turn.

Row 23: Color C, FLO sc second st from hook and 23 across, ch 1.

Rows 24–48: sc second st from hook and 23 across, ch 1, turn.

Left Panel

Rows 49–57: 16 sc, ch 1, turn.

Row 58: 16 sc across, (**do not** ch 1) turn.

Row 59: 8 sl st, ch 1, 8 sc, ch 1, turn.

Rows 60–63: 8 sc, ch 1, turn.

Right panel

Row 49: 8 sl st, ch 1, 16 sc, ch 1, turn.

Rows 50–58: 16 sc, ch 1, turn.

Rows 59–63: 8 sc, ch 1, turn.

Attach Front and Back Panels at shoulder and along sides, leaving 6" opening for arms.

COLLAR

Row 1: Color A, 53 sc around collar, ch 1, turn.

Rows 2–7: 53 sc, ch 1, turn.

Row 8: Color C, 53 sc, ch 1, turn.

Row 9: Color B, 53 sc. F/O

SLEEVES

Round 1: sl st to bottom of arm opening, ch 1, 39 sc around.
Rounds 2–3: 40 sc around.
Round 4: sc2tog, 38 sc around.
Round 5: sc2tog, 37 sc around.
Round 6: sc2tog, 36 sc around.
Round 7: sc2tog, 35 sc around.
Round 8: sc2tog, 34 sc around.
Rounds 9–40: 35 sc around.
Round 41: Color C, 35 sc around.
Round 42: Color B, 35 sc around.
Round 43: Color A, 35 sc around.

SIZE AGE 6

Repeat rows 1–7 at beginning one more time on back and front panels, this will increase length and add one more wave design.

SLEEVES

RRounds 1–50: 40 sc around.
Round 51: Color C, 40 sc around.
Round 52: Color B, 40 sc around.
Round 53: Color A, 40 sc around.

FLAG

Ch 16.
Rows 1–15: 15 sc across, ch 1, turn.
Sl st around flag with contrasting color.

SKULL

Round 1: ch 5, connect to first ch to form ring, ch 5, connect to same first ch.
Round 2: 8 sc in first ring, 8 sc in second ring (eyes).
Round 3: ch 3, connect with sc to first sc of first eye (forms nose), 15 sc around eyes, 4 sc in ch 3 space of nose. Sl st to next sc to fasten off.

BONES (Make 2)

Ch 3, sl st to first st, ch 3, sl st to same first chain.

Picture 4: Sc across.

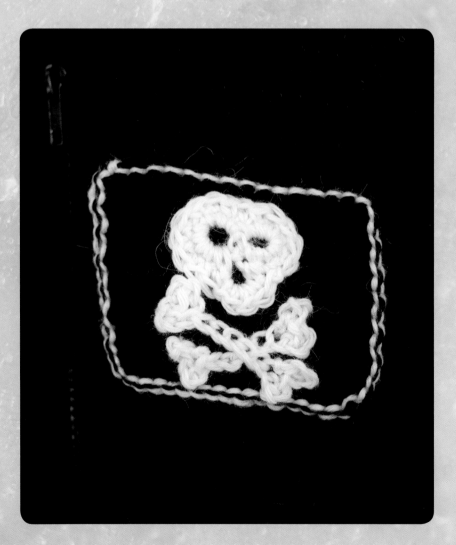

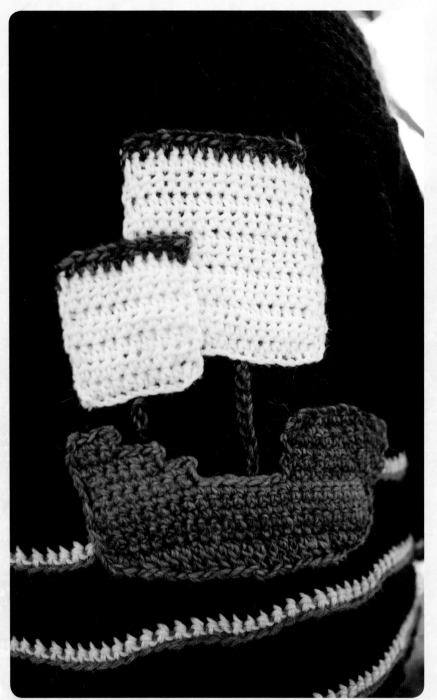

SHIP

Ch 25, turn.
Rows 1–5: 24 sc, ch 1, turn.
Rows 6–7: 8 sc, ch 1, turn.
Rows 8–9: 6 sc, ch 1, turn.
Rows 10–11: 3 sc, ch 1, turn.
Rotate so working down side of ship
11 sc down side.
Rotate so working across bottom
3 sc, 2 hdc, 15 dc, 2 hdc, 3 sc.
Rotate so working up opposite side
5 sc, ch 1.
Rotate so working across top of ship.
Row 6: 8 sc across, ch 1, turn.
Row 7: 8 sc across, 5 dc in last, ch 1, turn.
Row 8–11: 13 sc across, ch 1 turn.

SMALL SAIL

(White) ch 11.
Rows 1–7: 10 hdc, ch 1, turn.
Row 8: (Brown) 10 hdc.

LARGE SAIL

(White) ch 17.
Rows 1–10: 16 hdc across, ch 1, turn.
Row 11: (Brown) 16 hdc across.

MAST

Chain length desired.

Garden Jacket

This jacket was designed with my 4-year-old daughter in mind. She loves all the typical little girl things: rainbows, flowers, and 'tweet-tweet birds.' She has a fun fashion sense and is also very particular on what she wants to wear.

Materials

- Cascade Pima Silk 10x50g/109 yds 85% Peruvian Pima Cotton 15% Silk
  - Color #9212 / color name French Blue / 5 skeins (Color A)
  - Color #5225 / color name Fuschia / 2 skeins (Color B)
  - Color #9951 / color name Aqua / 2 skeins (Color C)
  - Color #3265 / color name Regal / 2 skeins (Color D)
  - Color #9293 / color name Emerald / 2 skeins (Color E)
- Zipper or buttons for closure. Size ages 4/5 jacket uses a 16" zipper. Make sure the zipper separates at the bottom.
- Hook: H (5mm)

Skill level: Intermediate

Gauge: Size 5mm hook, 8 Sc = 2", 8 Sc rows = 2"

Glossary of abbreviations

ch – chain
sc – single crochet
dc – double crochet
sc2tog – single crochet 2 together (decrease)
sl st – slip stitch
sk – skip
F/O – fasten off
(#) number of stitches at end of round
* _ * to be repeated

SIZE AGES 2/3

BACK

Color A, chain 46.
Rows 1–51: sc in second st from hook and 43 across, ch 1, turn.
Row 52: sc in second st from hook and 43 across, (DO NOT ch 1), turn.
Row 53: 10 sl st, sc in each of next 43 sts, leave last 10 unworked, ch 1, turn.
Rows 54–62: sc second st from hook and 31 sc across, ch 1, turn.
Rows 63–68: 8 sc across, ch 1, turn. F/O. Connect to opposite corner of row 63 with sl st, ch 1, 7 sc across, ch 1, turn.
Rows 63–68 (opposite side): 8 sc, ch 1, turn. F/O.

FRONT (Make two)

Color A, ch 25.
Rows 1–51: sc second st from hook and 27 across, ch 1, turn.

Row 52: sc second st from hook and 23 across, (DO NOT ch 1), turn.
Rows 53: 10 sl st, sc in each of next 14 sc, ch 1, turn.
Rows 54–62: sc 14 across, ch 1, turn.
Rows 63–68: 8 sc across, ch 1, turn. F/O. Attach Front and Back Panels.

SLEEVES

Round 1: (Color A) sl st to join, 50 sc around.
Round 2: (Color A) sc2tog, 49 sc around.
Round 3: (Color B) sc2tog, 48 sc around.
Round 4: (Color B) sc2tog, 47 sc around.
Round 5: (Color C) sc2tog, 46 sc around.
Round 6: (Color C) sc2tog, 45 sc around.
Round 7: (Color D) sc2tog, 44 sc around.
Round 8: (Color D) sc2tog, 43 sc around.
Round 9: (Color E) sc2tog, 42 sc around.
Round 10: (Color E) sc2tog, 41 sc around.

Round 11: (Color B) sc2tog, 40 sc around.
Round 12: (Color B) sc2tog, 39 sc around.
Rounds 13–50: 40 sc around, alternating colors B, C, D, E every two rows. F/O.

HOOD

Row 1: (Color A) sl st to middle of jacket at corner of one front panel. 63 sc across, ch 1, turn.
Row 2: (Color A) 63 sc across, ch 1, turn.
Rows 3–48: 73 sc across, ch 1, turn (alternating colors B, C, D, E every 2 rows)
Row 49: (Color E) 73 sc across. F/O.

SIZE AGES 4/5

BACK

Color A, Chain 56.

Rows 1–59: sc in second st from hook and 53 across, ch 1, turn.

Row 60: sc in second st from hook and 53 across, (DO NOT ch 1), turn.

Row 61: 10 sl st, sc in each of next 32 sts, leave last 10 unworked, ch 1, turn.

Rows 62–77: sc second st from hook and 31 sc across, ch 1, turn.

Rows 78–84: 8 sc across, ch 1, turn. F/O. Connect to opposite corner of row 78 with sl st, ch 1, 7 sc across, ch 1, turn.

Rows 79–84 (opposite side): 8 sc, ch 1, turn. F/O.

FRONT (Make two)

Color A, Chain 30.

Rows 1–59: sc second st from hook and 28 across, ch 1, turn.

Row 60: sc second st from hook and 28 across, (DO NOT ch 1), turn.

Row 61: 10 sl st, sc in each of next 19 sc, ch 1, turn.

Rows 62–76: sc in each of next 19 sc, ch 1, turn.

Rows 77–84: 8 sc across, ch 1, turn. F/O. Attach Front and Back Panels.

SLEEVES

Round 1: (Color A) sl St to join, 55 sc around.

Round 2: (Color A) sc2tog, 53 sc around.

Round 3: (Color B) sc2tog, 52 sc around.

Round 4: (Color B) sc2tog, 51 sc around.

Round 5: (Color C) sc2tog, 50 sc around.

Round 6: (Color C) sc2tog, 49 sc around.

Round 7: (Color D) sc2tog, 48 sc around.

Round 8: (Color D) sc2tog, 47 sc around.

Round 9: (Color E) sc2tog, 46 sc around.

Round 10: (Color E) sc2tog, 45 sc around.

Round 11: (Color B) sc2tog, 44 sc around.

Round 12: (Color B) 45 sc around.

Rounds 13–58: 45 sc around, alternating colors B, C, D, E every two rows. F/O.

HOOD

Row 1: (Color A) sl st to middle of jacket at corner of one front panel. 73 sc across, ch 1, turn.

Row 2: (Color A) 73 sc across, ch 1, turn.

Rows 3–56: 73 sc across, ch 1, turn (alternating colors B, C, D, E every 2 rows).

Row 57: (Color E) 73 sc across. F/O.

Spike Stitch
The Spike stitch is merely a single crochet placed a few rows below your working row.

GRASS TRIM
Color E, join with sl st at bottom corner of jacket.

Small Spike Stitch: Worked 2 rows above jacket bottom.

Large Spike Stitch: Worked 4 rows above jacket bottom.

Spike Stitch row: *2 sc, Small Spike stitch, 2 sc, Small Spike Stitch, 2 sc, Large Spike Stitch* repeat across bottom of jacket.

Picture 1: Insert hook a few rows below working row.

Picture 2: Yarn over hook.

Picture 3: Pull hook through working row.

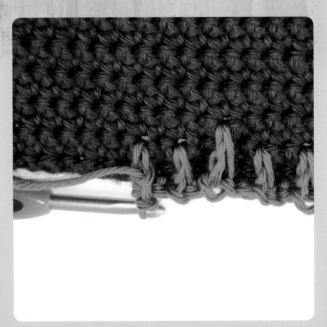
Picture 4: Yarn over and pull hook through all loops.

FLOWER
Round 1: ch 2, 5 sc in second st from hook. (5)
Round 2: 2 sc in each st around. (10)
Round 3: 2 sc in each st around. (20)
Round 4: 2 sc in each st around. (40)
Round 5: 2 sc in each st around. (80)
Round 5: 2 Sc in each st around (80)

BIRD
Round 1: ch 2, 8 sc in second st from hook.
Round 2: 2 sc in each st around.
Round 3: *2 sc in first, 1 sc next st* repeat 2 more times, hdc in each of next 2 sts, 2 dc in each of next 4 sts.

HEART WING (AND LEAF)
Start with ch 2, all of the following will be completed in second st from hook: 3 dc, ch 3, sl st, ch 3, 3 dc, join with sl st to first dc. F/O.

Toasty Tot Beanie and Scarf

This warm winter beanie and complementary scarf is sure to keep your child toasty during the cold winter months. By simply crocheting around the posts of the stitch, you'll create a ridged design. You can change colors every few rows or keep it the same color all the way through.

Materials

- Cascade Baby Alpaca Chunky 10 x 100g/108 yds 85% 100% Baby Alpaca
  – Color #592 / color name Olive Heather / 1 skein (Color A)
  – Color #585 / color name Stratosphere / 1 skein (Color B)
  – Color #580 / color name Ginger / 1 skein (Color C)
  – Color #568 / color name Emerald City / 1 skein (Color D)
  – Color #571 / color name Mahogany / 1 skein (Color E)
- Hook: I (5.5mm) for Hat and J (6mm) for Scarf

Skill level: Intermediate

Gauge: 2" circle at end of round 2 (16 FPhdc)

Glossary of abbreviations

ch – chain
sc – single crochet
dc – double crochet
sl st – slip stitch
sk – skip
hdc – half double crochet
FPhdc – Front Post half double crochet
F/O – fasten off
y/o – yarn over
(#) number of stitches at end of round
* _ * to be repeated (repeat)

Helpful Tips – Make color changes a last y/o of previous row.
The Front Post half double crochet will raise the previous round. (Picture 1)

BEANIE
TODDLER SIZE
(Circumference 16", Height 6")
Round 1: Color A, ch 2, 8 hdc in second st from hook. (8)
Round 2: Color B, 2 FPhdc in each st around. (16)
Round 3: Color C, *2 FPhdc in first st, 1 FPhdc in next st* repeat around. (24)
Round 4: Color D, *2 FPhdc in first st, 1 hdc in each of next 2 sts* repeat around. (32)
Round 5: Color E, * 2 FPhdc in first st, 1 FPhdc in each of next 3 sts* repeat around. (40)

Round 6: Color A, *2 hdc in first st, 1 hdc in each of next 4 sts* repeat around. (48)
Round 7: Color B, FPhdc around. (48)
Round 8: Color C, FPhdc around. (48)
Round 9: Color D, FPhdc around. (48)
Round 10: Color E, FPhdc around. (48)
Rounds 11–12: Color A, hdc around. (48)
Round 13: Color B, FPhdc around. (48)
Round 14: Color C, FPhdc around. (48)
Round 15: Color D, FPhdc around. (48)
Round 16: Color E, FPhdc around. (48)
Rounds 17–18: Color A, hdc around. (48)
Round 19: Color B, FPhdc around. (48)
Round 20: Color C, FPhdc around. (48)

Round 21: Color D, FPhdc around. (48)
Round 22: Color E, FPhdc around. (48)

CHILD SIZE
(Circumference 18", Height 7")
Round 1: Color A, ch 2, 8 hdc in second st from hook. (8)
Round 2: Color B, 2 FPhdc in each st around. (16)
Round 3: Color C, *2 FPhdc in first st, 1 FPhdc in next st* repeat around. (24)
Round 4: Color D, *2 FPhdc in first st, 1 hdc in each of next 2 sts* repeat around. (32)
Round 5: Color E, * 2 FPhdc in first st,

Picture 1: Close up of design.

Picture 2: Cut 4 pieces, 5" in length for each color.

Picture 3: Slip 3 pieces halfway through end of scarf.

Picture 4: Tie with fourth piece.

1 FPhdc in each of next 3 sts* repeat around. (40)

Round 6: Color A, *2 hdc in first st, 1 hdc in each of next 4 sts* repeat around. (48)

Round 7: Color A, *2 hdc in first st, 1 hdc in each of next 5 sts* repeat around. (56)

Round 8: Color B, FPhdc around. (56)

Round 9: Color C, FPhdc around. (56)

Round 10: Color D, FPhdc around. (56)

Round 11: Color E, FPhdc around. (56)

Rounds 12–13: Color A, hdc around. (56)

Round 14: Color B, FPhdc around. (56)

Round 15: Color C, FPhdc around. (56)

Round 16: Color D, FPhdc around. (56)

Round 17: Color E, FPhdc around. (56)

Rounds 18–19: Color A, hdc around. (56)

Round 20: Color B, FPhdc around. (56)

Round 21: Color C, FPhdc around. (56)

Round 22: Color D, FPhdc around. (56)

Round 23: Color E, FPhdc around. (56)

Rounds 24–25: Color A, hdc around. (56)

SCARF
Width 4", Length 54"

Color A, ch 161.

Row 1: Color A, hdc across, ch 1, turn.

Row 2: Color B, FPhdc across, ch 1, turn.

Row 3: Color B, hdc across, ch 1, turn.

Row 4: Color C, FPhdc across, ch 1, turn.

Row 5: Color C, hdc across, ch 1, turn.

Row 6: Color D, FPhdc across, ch 1, turn.

Row 7: Color D, hdc across, ch 1, turn.

Row 8: Color E, FPhdc across, ch 1, turn.

Row 9: Color E, hdc across, ch 1, turn.

Row 10: Color A, FPhdc across, ch 1, turn.

Row 11: Color A, hdc across, ch 1, turn.

Attach fringe to ends of scarf

(Pictures 2–4)

Acknowledgments and Size Chart

The gorgeous yarns used in this book were all supplied by **Cascade Yarns**, www.cascadeyarns.com.

I would like to extend a huge thank you to my husband and best friend, Jeff, for putting up with all of the yarn and for his support of this adventure! Thank you to all of the adorable models and their families involved with this book. I would also like to give special thanks to Angel Gray for jumping through hoops and creating amazing photographs that really showcased my designs and the fun-loving personalities of each model.

Tanya Bernard

SIZE CHART			
AGE	HEIGHT	WEIGHT	WAIST
2	34-37" 86-94 cm	29-32 lbs 13-14 kg	19-20" 48-50 cm
3	37-41" 94-104 cm	32-35 lbs 14-16 kg	19 ½-20½" 50-52 cm
4	41-45" 104-114 cm	35-38 lbs 16-17 kg	20-21" 50-53 cm
5	45-48" 114-122 cm	38-42 lbs 17-19 kg	21-22" 53-56 cm
6	48-51" 122-130 cm	42-46 lbs 19-21 kg	22-23" 56-59 cm